WITHDRAWN

DIGITAL
FABRICATION
IN ARCHITECTURE

LAURENCE KING

Published in 2012
by Laurence King Publishing Ltd
361–373 City Road
London EC1V 1LR
Tel +44 20 7841 6900
Fax +44 20 7841 6910
E enquiries@laurenceking.com
www.laurenceking.com

A catalogue record for this book is available from the British Library.

ISBN 978 185669 891 7
Designed by John Round Design
Printed in China

Front cover: Nordpark Cable Railway, Innsbruck, by Zaha Hadid © Roland Halbe

NICK DUNN

DIGITAL FABRICATION IN ARCHITECTURE

Laurence King Publishing

Contents

Related study material is available on the Laurence King website at
www.laurenceking.com

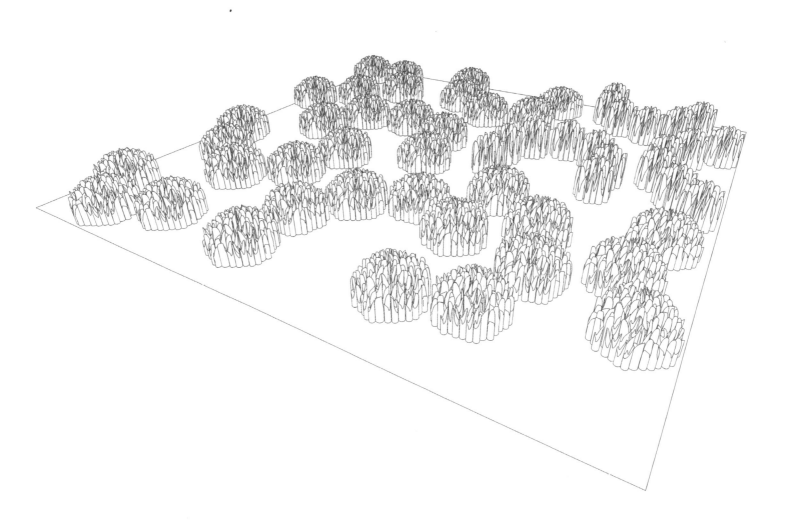

Introduction

Architecture is fundamentally concerned with two core activities: designing and making. Of course, these are not mutually exclusive and often inform one another in a continuous dialogue as projects progress from concepts, through design development to final form – typically the realization of a building. The ability to effectively communicate creative ideas remains a central aspect of the discipline. With the development of numerous Computer-Aided Design (CAD) and other software packages, the variety of design processes available to architects, which may influence the fabrication of architecture and its components, is greater than ever. Of specific interest in this field is the recent capability to integrate analogue and digital techniques and processes to produce physical objects, whether three-dimensional concept diagrams, scale models or full-size prototypes.

The increasing proliferation of computers and advanced modelling software has enabled architects and students alike to conceive and construct designs that would be very difficult to develop using traditional methods. In particular, the emergence of new computational modelling software, which allows parametric systems and complex 'biological' organizations to be generated and explored, offers new avenues of holistic design production and detailed component manufacturing for the architectural designer. These massive shifts in design processes have implications in material culture far beyond the discipline of architecture, as ever more research and development is conducted at cross-disciplinary levels worldwide. In addition, the application of CAD technologies as part of the production of physical models and prototypes is becoming increasingly widespread through processes such as CAD/CAM (Computer-Aided Manufacture), Computer Numerical Control (CNC) milling and rapid prototyping. The translation of computer-generated data to physical artefact is not a one-way street; processes may be reversed with equipment such as a three-dimensional scanner, or digitizer, which is used to trace contours of physical objects directly into the computer. Therefore, this book will focus on the inspiring possibilities offered by digital fabrication for architecture, with all the different technologies and techniques that are now available for the holistic and componential making of designs.

Above
The prevalence of digital images in the design and communication of architecture is commonplace. Even so, this imposes no limits on designers' creativity – as is shown by this digital montage for NOX's proposal for The Three Graces hotel and office towers in Dubai. The design is based on the idea of a 'networked' skin offering a symbolic gateway to the Khor Dubai Wharfage.

Above right
The pursuit by Supermanoeuvre of innovative design and fabrication processes is typified by Supermatter I, where a mould was first designed algorithmically. Fused Deposition Modelling was used to 3D print a positive so that a bronze cast could be produced via a lost mould process to form a complex self-supporting structure. Prototyping of this nature has significant potential for architecture as full structures may be realized from lightweight formwork.

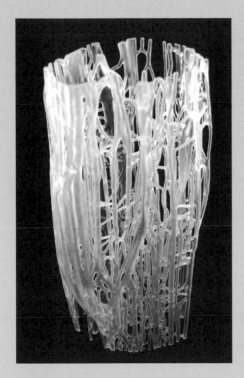

Above
This stereolithographic prototype of the skeletal structure for Kokkugia's project Fibrous Tower is part of a series of investigations that explore the generation of ornamental, structural and spatial order through an algorithmic design methodology. Conceived as a load-bearing shell that distributes forces across its network, the physical model is a direct translation of the sophisticated design data that satisfies such criteria.

Right
Zaha Hadid's Mobile Art Pavilion for Chanel takes advantage of digital imaging and construction processes to create a design with fluid geometries and dynamic space.

Below
Digital fabrication techniques provide architects with a spectrum of applications, transforming even long-held traditional methods of representation such as modelmaking. This digital model for Coop Himmelb(l)au's design for BMW Welt, Munich, was used to make laser-cut components to achieve its complex geometrical formal qualities.

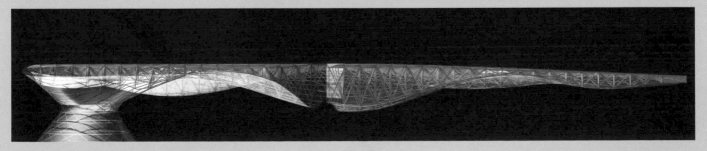

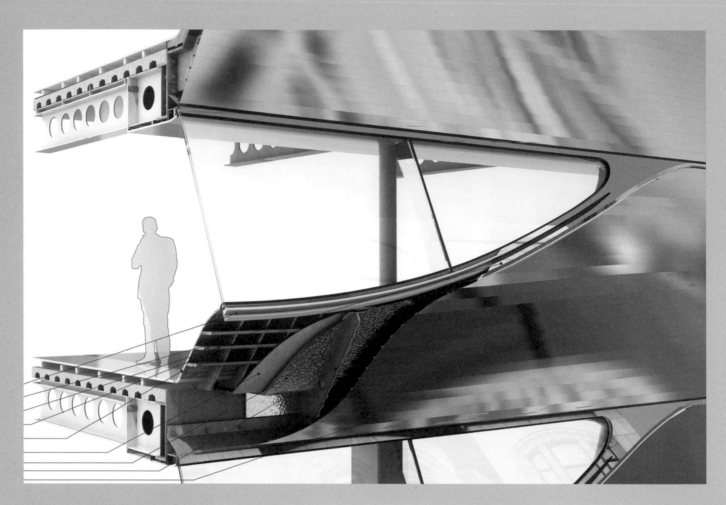

The design for Hills Place, London, by Amanda Levete Architects, developed this sculptural façade as a logical response to the narrow street, thereby maximizing the natural daylight available. The form is achieved through a system of aluminium profiles, more commonly used in the production of ship hulls. The façade is fabricated using curved 140mm profiles that are connected on site. The metallic silver coating is a high-performance paint typically applied to the surface of yachts. Self-cleaning glass and discreet hidden gutters ensure the façade retains its sculptural qualities.

Right

The architectural possibilities of developments in material technology continue to increase, fuelled by digital fabrication methods. For the Swarovski Crystal Palace, Greg Lynn FORM developed an installation utilizing cutting-edge technology from the nautical industry, in which carbon and aramid fibres are sandwiched between transparent Mylar™ sheets to produce a series of very strong yet lightweight 'sails' less than 1mm thick. With their potential application as spatial dividers or enclosures for future projects, the innovative design may provide a key stage for more research and development.

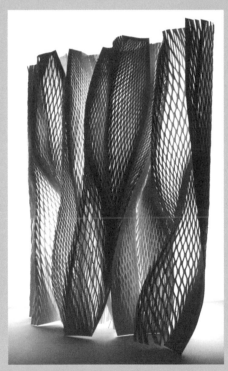

Above

Vector Wall by Reiser + Umemoto demonstrates the ways in which a laser cutter may be used to perforate a flexible or semi-flexible material with multidirectional patterning, reinterpreting the common wall. The model illustrated here was further developed as a full-size prototype to explore the potential application of the design and its adaptability. Refer to page 142 for how the project developed.

Above

Research into materials and their design opportunities informs the work of Barkow Leibinger – as shown in their speculative Coil Tubes. Using laser-cutting technology to form a spiralling pattern on a rotating steel tube, the subsequent geometry allows flexibility whilst segments also remain locked together. By the addition of LEDs into the tube, variable lighting effects are possible dependent on the degree of bending.

Left
Office for Metropolitan Architecture's (OMA) design for the China Central Television (CCTV) Headquarters proposed a digital media façade, allowing the building to display moving images and footage across its envelope.

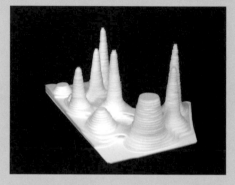

Left and above
The Gwanggyo Power Centre near Seoul, designed by MVRDV has been developed using a combination of digital design tools and manual model-making techniques. This hybrid process of creative flow between different modes of investigation is characteristic of the evolving nature of digital design in architecture.

Left
Foreign Office Architects' (FOA) seminal design for the Yokohama International Port Terminal, completed in 2002, coupled the concept of folded surfaces as circulation loops with the tectonic realization afforded by digital design tools.

Left
EMERGENT, founded by Tom Wiscombe, are renowned for synthesizing aesthetic and engineering issues into innovative design solutions, as shown in this laser-cut acrylic design-development model for the Garak Fish Market, Seoul, 2009.

Below
The screen façade design by San Francisco-based Faulders Studio for Airspace Tokyo – a collaboration with Studio M, Tokyo – illustrates the potential for digital design and fabrication methods to inform our built environment.

Above

The Energy Roof Perugia design by Coop Himmelb(l)au uses transparent photovoltaic cells to both produce energy and provide shading from the sun. The orientation of the individual cells is generated and optimized by a computer-driven scripting program.

Below left

UNStudio's design for the La Defense offices in Almere utilizes internal façades clad with glass panels, in which a multi-coloured foil is integrated and on to which – depending on the time of day and the angle of incidence – various different colours are reflected, animating the courtyards. This application of new materials to engage with users of the building and enliven the space is indicative of the ongoing development of material technology and its architectural implementations.

Below

University Library Utrecht by Wiel Arets Architects illustrates the manner in which materials may be worked within a digital design-and-production process to reinforce the twin concepts of 'openness' and 'protection'. In this image the façade components comprise opaque volumes and patterned glazing, to reduce sunlight penetration whilst offering legibility of the building's programme.

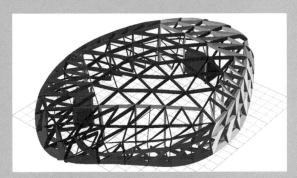

Above
The multidisciplinary design office ONL
(Oosterhuis_Lénárd) developed iWeb as
a mobile pavilion and interactive design
laboratory. Digital tools and fabrication
methods were used throughout the design
and realization processes, from initial concept,
through 3D structural strategies and CAD
renders, resulting in a full-size 'ProtoSpace'.

Below
Neri Oxman is an architect and researcher
whose work seeks to establish new forms of
experimental design and novel processes of
material practice at the interface of design,
computer science, material engineering
and ecology. Her Carpal Skin project is a
prototype for a glove to protect against
Carpal Tunnel Syndrome and is featured
in order to emphasize the multi-scalar
application of digital technologies.

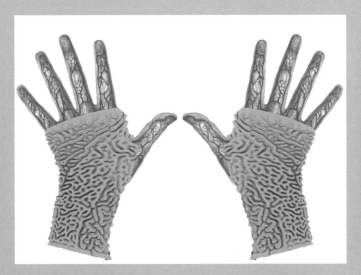

A brief history

Widespread availability, coupled with considerably reduced production costs, has afforded a growth in the use of computers unthinkable 20 years ago. That many of us engage unquestioningly with digital technologies on a daily basis provides some indication as to how easily, yet significantly, they have been assimilated into our everyday lives. Of course, it was not always thus. Indeed, even as recently as the early 1990s very few architectural practices used computers other than as timesaving devices for administrative tasks such as word processing and accounting. The design process was typically analogue, using traditional methods including freehand sketching, physical modelmaking, drawing on drafting boards, and manual final rendering techniques. Although computers were being used in other industries, early attempts to adopt them for architectural design, such as the Columbia University Paperless Studio project of 1992, were generally viewed as novel distractions rather than serious propositions for the future of design culture. Fast forward two decades and we find ourselves in a position where almost the reverse is true – we are almost unable to understand the design process of architecture *without* a degree of integration with digital technologies.

Architecture, of course, is not alone in this radical transformation, but before we begin to examine the potential of computers and digital technologies it is worth having a synoptic understanding of how we arrived at the contemporary situation. It is tempting to suggest that it was simply a matter of time before designers adopted technological developments, but this supposed inevitability belies a much more intricate series of historical events and societal changes. As Antoine Picon concludes, 'Technology is seldom the only explanation, especially in architecture where so much depends upon economic, social and cultural factors. The transformations that we are observing today. They are also the result of a much longer and complex historical process than the recent conversion of designers to digital tools.'[1]

It may be surprising to realize that the foundations for many present-day uses of digital technologies were laid at the turn of the nineteenth and twentieth centuries. A period typically referred to as the Second Industrial Revolution, this era witnessed a primary shift not only in modes of mass production and distribution of goods but also in the rise of information that supplemented these changes. As a consequence, the need to deal efficiently with all this data underscored the development of electric tabulating machines. Such machines evolved during the Second World War, giving birth to the computer as an advanced tool for handling huge quantities of information using mathematical logic, specifically binary operations, and the recent discoveries within electronic technologies to develop computability. The latter was of particular importance as it greatly increased the speed at which calculations and, by relation, information could be processed. These electronic calculators were vital for the military advancements made during the conflict. The ability of these early computers to control missile launches and trajectories alongside other increasingly complex weapon

1. Picon, A. (2010) *Digital Culture in Architecture: An Introduction for the Design Professions*. Birkhäuser, p.9.

Operator using the SAGE System interface.

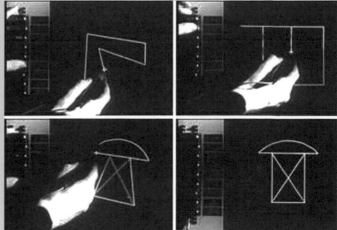

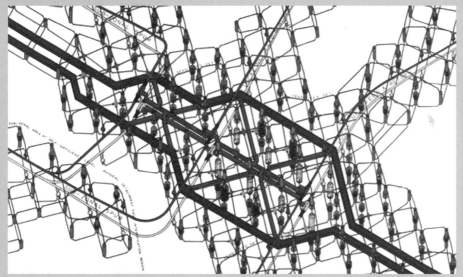

Above
Ivan Sutherland, with his early parametric CAD computer interface and screenshots, illustrating the use of the lightpen to change a design, 1963.

Left
Archigram's Computer City, the infrastructural networks that allowed Plug-In City to be more than an inert system of components, 1964.

systems meant that the enormous investment in such technologies bred further cutting-edge changes. The first computer network, the Semi-Automated Ground Environment (SAGE) System developed in the 1950s to coordinate radar operations, was one such advance. Inherent in such developments were innovations including video displays, artificial memories and information-translation processes that, after their initial inception in a military environment, would be integrated into commercially available systems.

Beyond this stage of computational development, a number of strands emerged which allowed this newfound technology to explore its limits. Significant here was the research and development into artificial intelligence and cybernetics, which negotiated the boundaries between the human and computer/machine interface. However, this was still primarily driven by a desire to optimize the people's capability in military scenarios. The relationship between humans and their environment is, of course, a fundamental preoccupation for architects, and so, with the advent of the new era ushered in with cybernetics, came a rich field of inquiry. In his influential article of 1969,

'The Architectural Relevance of Cybernetics', Gordon Pask outlined the potential for architects: 'The design goal is nearly always underspecified and the "controller" is no longer the authoritarian apparatus which this purely technical name commonly brings to mind. In contrast the controller is an odd mixture of catalyst, crutch, memory and arbiter. These, I believe, are the dispositions a designer should bring to bear upon his work (when he professionally plays the part of a controller) and these are the qualities he should embed in the systems (control systems) which he designs.'[2] This highlights one of the most important research themes during this period, that of efficiency. The ongoing experiments with cybernetics and systems theory were developed on the notion that informational processes formed patterns in nature and human endeavour that could be subsequently analyzed for strategic implementation within the built environment. This transformation was also occurring in the corporate field, wherein architecture was responding to the growing

2. Pask, G. 'The Architectural Relevance of Cybernetics',
Architectural Design, September 1969, p.496.

need for pattern-based designs to foster better performance within workplaces and corporate hierarchies. The resultant modularization of factory and, particularly, office designs began to span the apparent divide between the theoretically rigorous machinations of a corporate body and the social behaviour and patterns of individuals and small groups.

A key development in the evolution of the spatial nature of workplace planning was the design of the IBM System/360 by Eliot Noyes in the 1960s. This system comprised various modular components that could be organized in tandem with office furniture, and reflected the integrative manner in which IBM, amongst others, viewed the design of such space. This was further illustrated by the 'A Computer Perspective' exhibition, curated by Charles and Ray Eames and held at the IBM Corporate Exhibit Centre, New York, in 1971. Such events mirrored the increasing interrelationships between architecture and computer culture. In his Fun Palace project of 1960–1, British architect Cedric Price embraced cybernetic

theory as the principle upon which his design for a theatre and cultural centre would operate. Through collaboration with Gordon Pask, Price proposed a backstage computer that would offer a feedback loop between spectators and performers, facilitating an integrated system of continuous interaction. In 1976, Price subsequently developed his Generator Project, this time teaming up with John Frazer, a pioneer of artificial intelligence, to design a modularized system that was programmable and adaptable to its own environment owing to its built-in intelligence. Of course, whilst Price was one of the most forward-thinking architects of his time he was certainly not alone in his attempts to engage architecture with computer technology.

In Paris, Yona Friedman had, since 1958, been exploring the possibilities of The Spatial City, a vast megastructure or architectural 'circuit board', across which elements could be added, removed or enhanced. This theory would be developed during the late 1960s in his design for Flatwriter,

Right
Gordon Pask's Colloquy of Mobiles for the 'Cybernetic Serendipity' exhibition held at the ICA in London, 1968. Conceived as a reactive, educable, computer-based system comprising five mobiles, the installation enabled visitors to have a 'conversation' with the machines by using lights and mirrors to activate the rotating mobiles.

Below right
An IBM 360 mainframe computer in use, late 1960s. The modularization of the system's components allowed easy assimilation into the office environment.

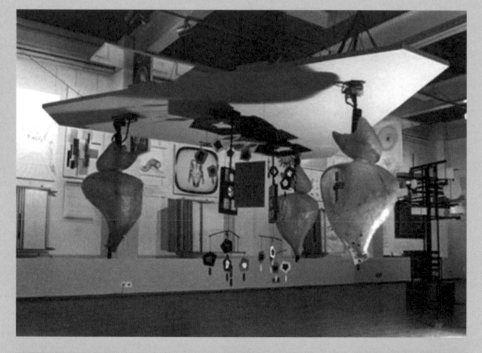

John and Julia Frazer's Generator interface, developed in collaboration with Cedric Price, 1976–80.

a computerized system that enabled individual inhabitants of a city to imprint their personal preferences with respect to their apartments, and by using symbols to reference the different elements of these decisions the builder, as well as their neighbours, could understand the choices made. In the United States, Nicholas Negroponte founded the Architecture Machine Group at the Massachusetts Institute of Technology (MIT) in 1967. Through his directive to explore the interface between human and machine, typified in seminal papers such as 'Towards a Humanism through Machines' in 1969, one of the research strands the group pursued addressed the relationships between humans and computers. This objective eventually gave rise to the Media Lab, which continues to push the boundaries of innovation and experimentation with regard to digital technologies and architecture today.

Meanwhile back in the UK, the avant-garde group Archigram were keen to absorb the latest technological advances into their Pop Art and science-fiction explosion of arresting imagery and provocative ideas. Indeed, the polemic of one of their most influential projects, Plug-In City, 1964, was given further impetus by the novelty of its power source: the 'Synthesised Metropolis With Electronic Changeability', aka Computer City. The key feature of this project was its depiction of computer technology not merely as a representational tool but as an environmental model. In Dennis Crompton's words: 'The activities of an organized society occur within a balanced network of forces which naturally interact to form a continuous chain of change. A METROPOLIS is situated at the point of maximum display of interactive energy and shows the most complex field of forces. In the COMPUTOR [*sic.*] CITY this energized field is synthesized at a much higher sensitivity and is programmed to respond to changes in activity.'[3] The contours of Computer City therefore comprised not

information but how information moved from one place to another. Although this was a conceptual project that did not directly involve itself with technology beyond illustrative implications, it signalled an important movement that was occurring internationally as architects sought to address the emerging presence and potential of the computer in society. This position was taken to its logical conclusion in Archigram's later project, Instant City, 1968–70, which examined prevailing attitudes regarding city centres in relation to networks. As Hadas Steiner has observed, 'the urban experience of Instant City was shifting toward a point where information and the city were synonymous. In its ideal form, Instant City would provide a bundle of services; its urban strategy would be connectivity and speed over geographical advantage. To inhabit an advanced network, information and the city would be fully decentralized commodities that travelled the same infrastructure, like computers on phone lines.'[4] This essentially describes the contemporary situation of many cities worldwide, wherein the physical urban landscape is augmented by digital networks, and was particularly prescient.

Architectural history books describe the late 1960s and early 1970s as a very rich time for cultural experimentation, and attempts to embrace computers into this mix were also manifold. The introduction of the Internet into the public domain and the mass consumption of personal computers during the 1980s and 1990s, led to an increasing prevalence of computer technology in everyday lives. The effects of this ubiquitous technology upon the individual in society was

3. Crompton, D. *Archigram 5*, Autumn 1964.

4. Steiner, H. A. (2009) *Beyond Archigram: The Structure of Circulation.* Routledge, p.217.

discussed in Nicholas Negroponte's *Being Digital*: 'As we interconnect ourselves, many of the values of a nation-state will give way to those of both larger and smaller electronic communities. We will socialize in digital neighborhoods in which physical space will be irrelevant and time will play a different role.'[5] Parallel to this was the ongoing investigation into the capacity of computers to drive architectural design. In more radical research areas, this was not simply a case of computers imitating what humans could already do but actually replacing them within the design process. As John Frazer outlines in his widely regarded *An Evolutionary Architecture*, 'Architectural concepts are expressed as generative rules so that their evolution may be accelerated and tested. The rules are described in a genetic language which produces a code-script of instructions for form-generation. Computer models are used to simulate the development of prototypical forms which are then evaluated on the basis of their performance in a simulated environment. A very large number of evolutionary steps can be generated in a short space of time, and the emergent forms are often unexpected.'[6]

This leads us towards the contemporary situation, in which architecture and computers are frequently synonymous. From conceptual design to manufacturing and on-site assembly, computers and digital technologies have transformed not only the way we *represent* our ideas but also the means through which we *generate* them. A range of digital tools is now available: explorative ones allow the designer to investigate emergent concepts via novel computation and generative form finding; descriptive ones, such as three-dimensional modelling and visualization, enable us to understand a design and its development; predictive and evaluative analytical tools allow designers to test the implications and performance of design ideas; and some tools even act as part of the final production of building elements and coordination of construction. It is the last aspect that provides this book's central focus. However, we will also discuss some of the other interdependent and beneficial approaches to digital technology's use in architectural design and production. Digital fabrication, therefore, is typically, but not always, a later stage of the design process, and as the name suggests, it is a method using digital data to direct a manufacturing process. That does not mean it follows a conventional route and that design results in the pushing of a button to make something – in fact, nothing could be further from the truth! Many of the fabrication processes featured here require the designer to consider the elements to be fabricated much earlier in the ideation stage.

5. Negroponte, N. (1995) *Being Digital*. Alfred A. Knopf, p.7.

6. Frazer, J. (1995) *An Evolutionary Architecture*. Architectural Association, p.9.

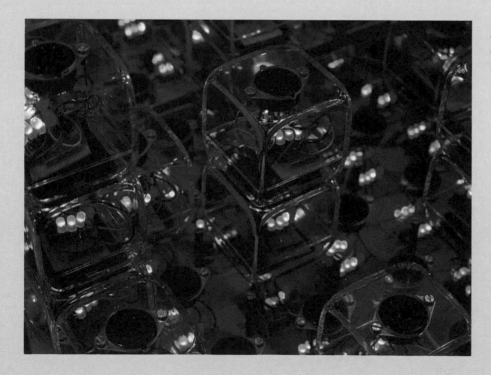

Detail from the Universal Constructor, a working model of a self-organizing interactive environment made as a group project led by John Frazer, 1990.

Left

The transformational nature of digital technologies is prevalent in a range of architectural projects, such as the iconic Blur Building, Yverdon-les-Bains, built for the Swiss 2002 Expo. Literally an 'architecture of atmosphere', the design uses an intelligent weather system to read varying climactic conditions – temperature, humidity, wind speed and direction – and processes this data in a computer to regulate the water pressure of the 'fog' accordingly.

Below

A key aspect of digital technologies is interactivity. This interface, developed by Coop Himmelb(l)au for their Brain City Lab project, allows visitors to act as emitters or attractors of information within the installation so that their position and movement directly influence the information flow within the virtual city, producing new connections and centres.

Bottom

Design and manufacturing processes from other disciplines are being integrated with architecture to develop innovative methods of constructing complex geometrical elements. VoltaDom is an installation designed by Skylar Tibbits for MIT's 150th Anniversary Celebration & FAST Arts Festival, 2011. The project expands the notion of the architectural 'surface panel' by intensifying the depth of a doubly curved vaulted surface, while maintaining relative ease in assembly and fabrication. This is made possible by transforming complex curved vaults into developable strips. The assembly could be likened to simply rolling a strip of material.

Fabricating architecture in the digital age

Digital fabrication in architecture is a relatively recent phenomenon, emerging over the last 15 years to become a substantial aspect of critical debate, professional practice and education within the discipline. Essentially, it is a sub-category of Computer-Aided Design and Computer-Aided Manufacturing (CAD/CAM) since it utilizes computer-controlled machines as tools with which to cut or make parts. Whilst still relatively novel in architecture, CAD/CAM processes have been used in engineering and industrial design for over 50 years in the development and fabrication of cars, aeroplanes and smaller consumer goods. Components are usually designed and developed with three-dimensional modelling software, and then scale models are produced using a rapid protoyping process that translates digital information into physical object. Because this type of object includes all the data from the computational model, it is often highly detailed and therefore provides a precise description of the design. This stage may be reiterated to revise the design until such a point is reached that full-size prototypes are made, either as parts in themselves or to form moulds from which components are subsequently made; in either scenario, a variety of materials may be used depending on the intended purpose.

More importantly, this process has facilitated a greater fluidity between design generation, development and fabrication than in traditional approaches, which necessitated a more cumulative, staged process. The potential to make things directly from design information has precipitated a transformation in design disciplines, as it allows the designer to engage with the entire process from concept to final product in an unprecedented manner. A significant figure in the field, Lisa Iwamoto describes this shift: '[F]or many years, as the process of making drawings steadily shifted from being analog to digital, the design of buildings did not really reflect the change. CAD replaced drawings with a parallel rule and lead pointer, but buildings looked pretty much the same. This is perhaps not so surprising – one form of two-dimensional representation simply replaced another. It took three-dimensional computer modeling and digital fabrication to energize design thinking and expand the boundaries of architectural form and construction.'[7]

7. Iwamoto, L. (2009) *Digital Fabrications: Architectural and Material Techniques.* Princeton Architectural Press, p.5.

The Disney Concert Hall, Los Angeles, by Frank O. Gehry & Associates. Perhaps one of the most important architectural projects with regard to digital technologies, it fuelled the development of their application in the discipline, generating specific software programs in the process as well as demonstrating their potential to a wider audience.

Right
Digital design software has proved a valuable tool for analyzing the performance of different architectural elements, for example in the design development of the external-skin panels for the Heydar Aliyev Cultural Centre, Baku, by Zaha Hadid.

Below right
Ongoing developments in digital 3D modelling software have produced specific platforms and bespoke plug-ins to enable complex designs to be readily translated for digital fabrication, as illustrated in this screenshot of cutting patterns for the Aurora project by Future Cities Lab.

Bottom
Batwing, a prototype developed by EMERGENT/ Tom Wiscombe as part of a larger body of work concerned with creating coherent relationships between building systems through geometric and atmospheric means.

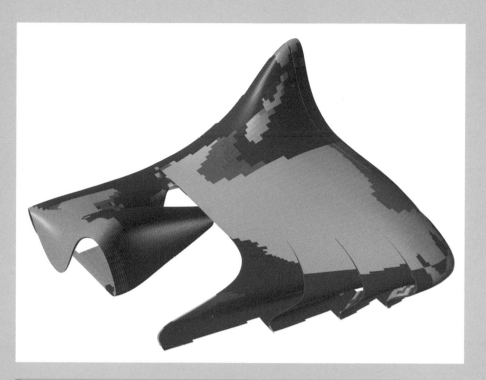

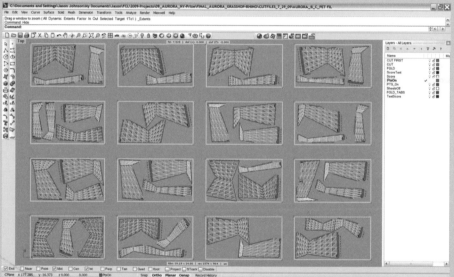

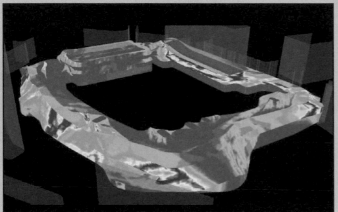

Top
The cladding for Birmingham New Street
Station by FOA will be built as a stainless-
steel skin that conceals future plant areas on
the roof and wraps around the existing car
park. As the cladding cannot, for practical
reasons, be related to the building's interior,
the façade responds to the exterior space,
making the building an instrument for
intensifying the perception of urban life.

Above left
Technical software produces glare studies
for the project. Here, accumulation glare
is mapped on to the south-east façades,
enabling the designers to refine the
articulation of the geometry as appropriate.

Above right
A full-size mock-up panel of the stainless-steel
cladding system affords further development
and detailed evaluation of the proposed design
in both technological and aesthetic terms.

The transformations accompanying digital fabrication
have typically grown from specific projects, in which
design aspirations and corresponding technological
innovations have pushed the development of software and
manufacturing processes beyond conventional boundaries.
An early advocate of such an approach was Gehry &
Associates, whose adoption and development of digital
tools was vital in enabling them to construct the highly
complex geometry of their designs. Indeed, a watershed
project in this regard was the iconic Disney Concert Hall,
1989–2003, which required the implementation of CAD/
CAM technology for its design and production. Already
heavily reliant on physical model-making techniques to
develop their intricate designs, the practice initially used
such models in conjunction with a 3D digitizer to feed data
into the computer, initiating a dialogue between analogue
and digital models to refine the design. The critical part
of this translation process lay in the practice's adaptation
of an existing software program, Computer-Aided Three-
dimensional Interactive Application (CATIA). An established
design-and-development platform within the aerospace
industry, CATIA was employed here to model the building's
envelope and permitted full-size prototypes to be digitally
fabricated, as data was used from the digital models to
control machines that cut stone to the required geometries.

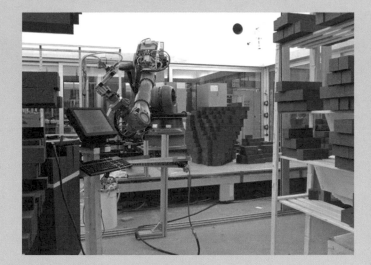

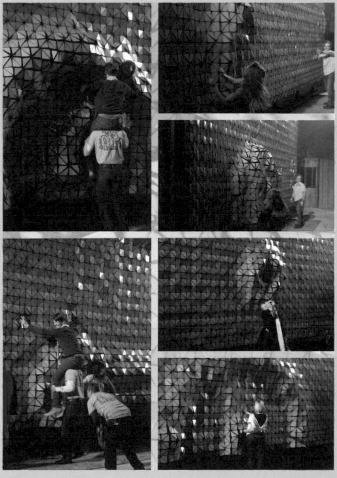

Through such developments, digital technologies have advanced the architectural discourse. Not that these kinds of changes are exclusive to the discipline – quite the reverse, as the continual evolution of design, analysis and production processes attests, challenging and augmenting existing procedures and organizations across the design and construction industries. The impetus provided by technological advances has traditionally served to improve protocols within these industries and, whilst certainly awe-inspiring, it is important to realize that digital tools and methods have resulted in further integration with extant techniques rather than less, as Branko Kolarevic observes: 'It is intriguing to note that this emerging, technologically enabled transformation of the building industry in the "digital" age has led to a much greater integration of "mechanical" age processes and techniques into conceptual building design.'[8] However, perhaps one of most exciting developments in this arena is the accessibility of digital design and fabrication technologies to architectural practitioners and students. Therefore, it is worth considering what we are trying to achieve before we immerse ourselves in these technologies.

Top left
The nature and processes of making in architectural design are evolving at an unprecedented rate. Architects are keen to develop cross-disciplinary avenues of exploration from other industries – for example, this robot from the automotive sector – to test their application and opportunities.

Above
Not only is the way we manufacture components and buildings transforming our design ideas, but their material possibilities may now also be realized like never before. The HypoSurface, developed by Mark Goulthorpe/ dECOi, is an ongoing project exploring a dynamic and interactive architectural surface and has an immediate plastic reciprocity that responds to the actions of people, challenging the typically static nature of architectural form.

8. Kolarevic, B. & Klinger, K. [eds.] (2008) *Manufacturing Material Effects: Rethinking Design and Making in Architecture.* Routledge, p.7.

About this book

This book is organized into three sections. The first covers the wide spectrum of digital technologies now available. It will demonstrate the range of tools accessible to the architect/ student when developing and communicating their designs from initial concept to final presentation, and how these underpin new approaches in making. This section will explore these tools' implications upon the design process and describe their performative properties in terms of translating digital information into manufactured elements across a range of scales, whether as fully integrated building systems or specific components. Furthermore, it will analyze the active role of the computer within the design process and examine a number of research strands pursuing novel methods of design generation and development. The second section will build upon this information and describe the variety of methods whereby digital data generated during the design process may be integrated with fabrication techniques to provide exciting and innovative processes with which designers may further refine and communicate their ideas. This area is one of significant transformation across a number of design disciplines, including architecture, and this section will therefore discuss the various attributes of different approaches and techniques to consolidate understanding for the designer prior to implementation. The third section will concentrate on those strategies through which the generation and integration of design ideas with fabrication processes may be employed in a coherent and explorative manner. This section will place significant emphasis on design by computational manipulation rather than determinism, to afford more experimental and speculative approaches to problems. It will describe and evaluate a range of advanced tooling procedures in terms of their application in architecture. It will then describe the various implications for the materiality of ideas as they become transformed from bundles of data to real objects. Therefore, this section extends the knowledge of the previous two into a more specialist field, permitting designers to be more discerning in their selection and use of particular techniques. Throughout the book, case studies demonstrate how a range of aspects and techniques from each section may be combined to produce innovative architectural design. By describing and explaining these different approaches and their skilful handling in an integrated digital design process and fabrication method, the case studies enhance readers' understanding of those sections of the book whilst unveiling just some of the many possibilities through which such techniques may be applied.

Many of the projects featured illustrate highly innovative and experimental designs generated or fabricated through digital processes, sometimes as a fluid workflow between conception and production. In order to provide the reader with an appropriate balance of techniques and subject matter, this book includes work from established practices alongside emerging designers and architects. The relative affordability of digital design and fabrication technologies has brought them within the grasp of professionals and students alike, and a number of student projects are featured here to emphasize the pioneering work and 'do-it-yourself' ethos that they represent. Ultimately, with these technologies continuing to evolve and inform the future of architectural design, this book aims to inspire the next generation of designers and help them develop their creative ideas with the potential of digital fabrication.

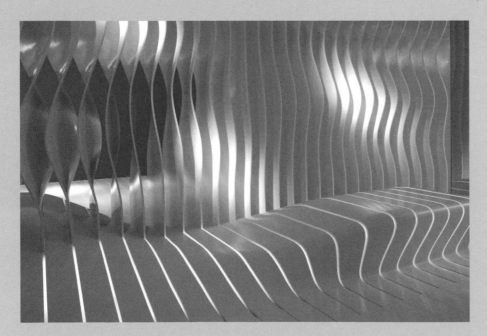

Amanda Levete Architects designed the Corian® Lounge, which used advanced digital technology in its design process as well as for fabrication – specifically, development of an adjustable mould that enabled efficiency and variability in component production.

Getting started

The innovative and experimental opportunities inherent in digital fabrication are myriad and exciting, so the first question that confronts a designer may be simply: where do I begin? There are no hard and fast rules about when to use digital tools and technologies for architectural design – or, indeed, which tools to use – and given the overwhelming amount of different techniques available to the designer it may often appear a daunting premise. This is particularly pertinent where inexperienced designers seek to engage with complex computer software, which rather than assisting or even driving their design ideas appears to do the opposite, thereby limiting creativity and sometimes resulting in considerable frustration! Therefore, it is important to understand from the outset that these methods form part of a more expansive 'toolkit' for architectural design which also includes traditional modes of inquiry and representation such as sketching, drawing, physical modelmaking and painting. It is not the intention here to curb any ambition on behalf of the designer – quite the reverse – but to understand that there are different degrees to which these techniques may be used within a design process. The seductive aspects of some of the digital technologies featured may imply a mere 'touch of a button' approach to design, but the reality of investment in terms of time, effort and cost should not be ignored.

Perhaps the most obvious shift in the behaviour of a designer using digital fabrication techniques lies at the very core of making. In order to be able to fabricate something, we need to first convert digital data from design software into a format that CAD/CAM machines can understand. This necessitates designers developing a degree of understanding as to how these translation processes work, so they may best exploit the machines' capabilities.

One of the objectives of this book, therefore, is to enable those designers seeking to incorporate digital technologies into their practice, whether partially or comprehensively, to be more discriminating in their choice of appropriate tools. Clearly, this is a skill that improves with experience, and with the wealth of approaches accessible to designers experimentation is also strongly encouraged – albeit grounded in a basic understanding of *how* these tools and processes work, *why* they are useful and *when* they may be appropriate in the context of architectural design.

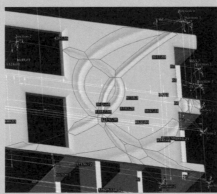

Above and above right
This early conceptual freehand sketch by Ilona Lénárd of ONL for the F Zuid housing in Amsterdam was quickly developed to form a pattern that was wrapped around the buildings' façades. Parametric modelling enabled the surface pattern to be optimized around the external envelope.

Above
Innovative connection components made using a 3D printing rapid-prototyping process by the Nonlinear Systems Biology and Design workshop group led by Jenny Sabin and Peter Lloyd Jones at SmartGeometry, Barcelona. The form of the nodes mutates to generate various spatial conditions when connected together with flexible, tubular components.

Digital tools and machines for fabrication

It is not the purpose of this book to provide comprehensive knowledge of the extensive range of software programs available to designers. Rather than present an onerous amount of information that may rapidly become obsolete, the approach taken here is to outline principles and methods of working with different types of software. These general overviews are intended to complement software-specific manuals and technical guides, as well as the myriad online resources and tutorials. Similarly, the use of CAD/CAM machinery will initially require some investment in learning the various protocols and conversion software – either through self-direction or, more likely, under the supervision of a trained operator or workshop technician. That is not to say a novice designer should be intimidated by digital tools and machines, and to reassure those beginning their journey into this new world it may be comforting to know that these technologies are already being embraced in the public domain. Through ongoing initiatives such as the Fab Lab programme, developed as part of MIT's Center for Bits and Atoms, digital fabrication techniques are already firmly in the hands of design communities and the public in cities worldwide, and interest in these methods is quickly becoming widespread and networked.

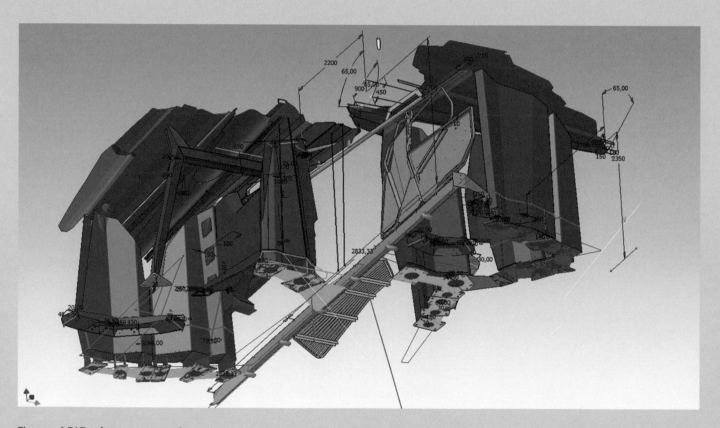

The use of CAD software to accurately develop design intentions is commonplace in architecture schools and offices alike. However, its role as a tool with which to create bespoke designs and generate information for CAD/CAM processes – as illustrated by this drawing for the 55/02 shelter, Northumbria, designed by sixteen*(makers) – is increasingly prevalent.

Computer-Aided Design

A multitude of different software programs is available to the designer, and selection often comes from personal preferences in relation to the usability of the software's interface alongside more pragmatic issues such as the technical capability of the program. Computer-Aided Design is an umbrella term, covering a considerable range of programs that share a number of common features but also have particular characteristics for specialist applications. The most widely known packages for architecture are: AutoCAD, MicroStation and VectorWorks.

3D modelling software

A subsidiary of CAD software, these programs have been especially designed for three-dimensional modelling and visualization. Whilst some of the general CAD platforms, such as those listed above, will address most designers' needs, there are several key programs in general use within practice and architecture schools: 3ds Max, Google SketchUp, MAYA and Rhino.

Generative or parametric software

Generative design is a further subset of modelling software and indeed may even use additional computer scripts or programs, referred to as 'plug-ins', to augment 3D modelling software. Again, personal criteria may influence choice here, but the most commonly used programs are: Digital Project, GenerativeComponents, Grasshopper, MAX script, MEL script and Processing.

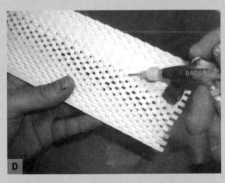

A The use of digital fabrication machines is typically facilitated by the machine's software interface, which may require some additional learning on behalf of the user to obtain the best results from the production processes.

B Laser-cutting machine, useful for detailed model or prototype components cut from thick paper, cardboard, acrylic sheet, thin metal sheets, slim wooden veneers or composite sheets.

C Rapid Prototyping machine, in this case a Z-Starch version, that builds up layers using a powder which is bonded together.

D Typically adjacent to rapid-prototyping equipment is a machine that allows the designer to clean off any excess powder using specific tools in a controlled environment.

E AND F CNC router, one of the more typical configurations that utilizes a gantry to enable the cutting head to move across the machine bed (left). These machines are often controlled by a handheld keypad, as shown right.

Above

In contrast to the gantry type, this version of a CNC router has an enclosed environment and may be used to cut thin sheet metal and plastics as well as wood.

Above right

CNC milling machine removing material from timber sheet. The difference between milling and routing relates to the type of drill bit attached to the cutting head, but the overall apparatus is typically identical.

Below

A rapid-prototyped model, produced using the Selective Laser Sintering method.

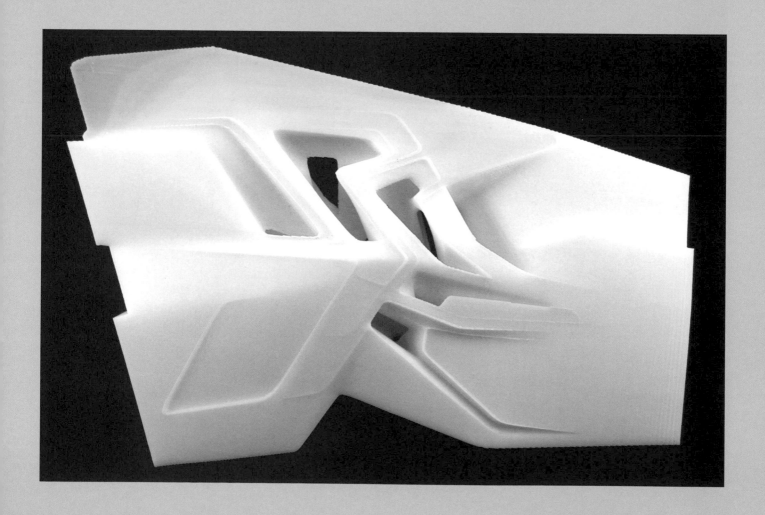

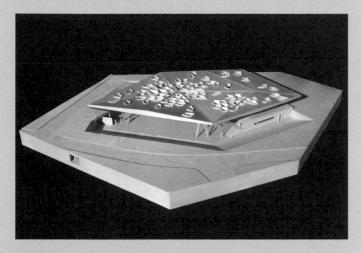

Above

The technological developments that have afforded digital fabrication in architecture have once again brought the architect much closer to the processes of making. The increasing need to understand the implications of the design data, since this is also often the construction data, is a key factor in contemporary practice. Barkow Leibinger's design for the Campus Restaurant, shown here as a model and under construction, was developed through a rigorous approach to material properties and production methods.

Below

The work of Studio Gang reflects their interdisciplinary approach to architecture and design, exploring ideas across a range of scales from cities to specific material inquiries and components. Their award-winning design for the Aqua Tower in Chicago demonstrates a seamless transition from CAD design to physical production.

PART I GENERATION

1. Introduction

Prior to engaging with physical materials, any aspiring designer must understand the various ways in which digital information is composed to be used at a later stage to make things. Therefore, this first section will describe the various geometries behind digital technologies and contextualize the new tools that allow the architectural practitioner to generate and communicate innovative design ideas. The implications of these design and visualizing methods as part of the making process will be discussed with reference to innovative examples. This will underscore the following sections of the book, covering how to approach the fabrication of models, prototypes and other objects from a digital perspective. The roles of contemporary and emergent computational processes in handling data, and their characteristic features in terms of design intentions and material expression, will be analyzed and discussed. With the increased proliferation of computers, designers are faced with a myriad of possible tools; this section will clarify the different purposes of various processes, to enable selection of appropriate technologies. Of primary interest is the shift occurring through the use of digital technologies in construction processes, which in turn influences the way architects are learning and practising. This development is transformative as we evolve out of the information age, in which digital technology drove the possibilities for creativity, to a situation wherein our ideas are pushing the boundaries of such technologies, facilitating further innovation and exploration. Before delving deeper into the approaches and cutting-edge techniques becoming more popular in architecture schools and practices, we need to consider how we make our ideas digitally – and this leads us to the first area of discussion, CAD geometry.

Below

CAD software's ability to produce stunning visualizations of proposed projects – such as this Coop Himmelb(l)au design for the Busan Cinema Centre – is perhaps its most widely understood application, but the capability and integration of computers within the architectural design process is ever-expanding.

Bottom right

In addition to overall views and general-arrangement drawings, CAD is particularly valuable for 3D modelling of specific details – providing a clear understanding of how components connect, as shown in this structural-node detail for the Leadenhall Building, London, by Rogers Stirk Harbour + Partners. The node geometry and connections are exported directly from the Building Information Management (BIM) model, allowing designers to see the implications of any changes to the detail.

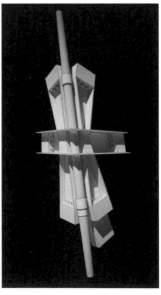

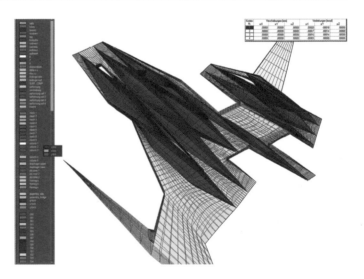

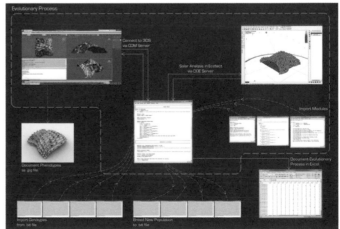

Above

Rather than simply enabling manual tasks to be replicated, CAD software has developed to a stage where the imagination of the user may generate and express designs that would be difficult to achieve in traditional representational methods. The beauty and complexity of Joanna Szulda's design for a Natural Childbirth and Women's Centre embraces the potential of such software to explore sensual and emotional aspects of explorative spatial configurations through texture, colour and pattern.

Right

EMERGENT/Tom Wiscombe's design for the MoMA/P.S.1 Urban Beach, New York, was based on two primary elements: a cellular roof and leisure landscape. The roof design was developed via the creation of a long-span structure through the use of a non-hierarchical structural patterning of distinct but interlaced units or cells, as shown in this screenshot.

Bottom right

The translation and flow of data between programs is a key aspect of digital design and fabrication. This screenshot of a speculative pavilion by Daniel Richards is from Python, an open-source programming language, and facilitates an effective interface between a CAD program (3Ds Max) and analysis software (Ecotect) – and then documentation of the process with Microsoft Excel and JPEG images.

2. CAD

Computer-Aided Design (CAD) software is now so ubiquitous in architecture schools and practices that we rarely question its presence – indeed, many cannot even imagine a time when it was not part of our design 'toolkit'. As an umbrella term, CAD covers a vast array of programs that produce different results. Some only create two-dimensional drawings, whilst others are capable of highly sophisticated three-dimensional renders and animations. The initial benefits of CAD principally related to its suitability for repetitive work, as it facilitated the use of 'copy', 'cut' and 'paste' functions. These generic tasks enable a designer to very quickly add, reposition or remove elements of the design by selecting the appropriate part(s) and then carrying out the required function, typically through an on-screen menu. These functions raise an interesting issue that will have greater implications further on in this section, that of *independence*. The simple fact that design elements can be so easily manipulated is due to their independent nature, i.e. even though they may appear visually connected to other elements within the design they are not, so if one element is moved then those surrounding it remain unaffected. This functionality of CAD software affords rapid construction and transformation of designs through simple stages. In order to position elements relative to each other, CAD users set up grids or guidelines as a background layer to the drawing to enable them to connect or 'snap' the elements together effectively. However, this behaviour also highlights one of the disadvantages of the independent nature of this technique, since making significant changes to the drawing may result in many other parts also having to be copied, repositioned or pasted. Clearly, the

Below
Revit screenshot from ONL's drawing package for the Al Nasser Group headquarters, Abu Dhabi. The tower's gently curving form renders each floor unique, which makes the use of digital design tools very pragmatic.

Bottom right
Photorealistic computer-generated images (CGIs) are frequently used to sell the potential of a design prior to development, and may be advanced and detailed enough for it to be difficult to know exactly what is real and what is virtual – as shown in this image for Rogers Stirk Harbour + Partners' design for the Leadenhall Building, London.

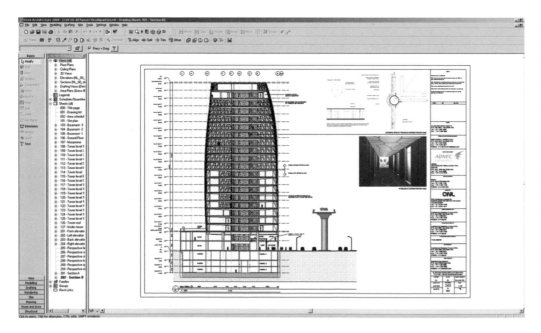

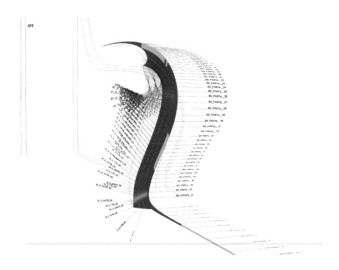

greater the degree of complexity in the CAD drawing, the more manual work involved in revising it. As such, CAD programs based on this type of functionality are very useful once a design is well developed, but may limit early exploration and constrain the design process.

One of the primary benefits of CAD data is its transferability into other software platforms and formats. The majority of computer-generated images (CGI) readily used in architecture and in the visual encounters of our everyday lives – such as advertising, television, films, animations – are not simply the product of one single software program but are hybridized images that were developed using numerous packages to optimize their visual impact. However, once the final images are produced there remains the fundamental process of showing how the objects can be constructed within a CAD environment. A key issue in using any CAD software prior to fabrication is scale. It is important for any designer to consider the limits of the machine they intend to use since there will be constraints in terms of the size and number of elements it can make at any one time. Herein, we discern the need for geometry to create, manipulate and refine our design ideas. In contrast to physical modelmaking – through which we manually alter the shape, form and geometry of a material depending on its properties – in a CAD setting we are unable (yet!) to literally reach into the screen and directly change a surface or form. We therefore need suitable mechanisms by which we may control appearance and other formal characteristics. This is where the geometry of CAD software comes to the fore, as it affords the designer a level of command over creative ideas. There are two basic ways of making three-dimensional forms digitally: Non-Uniform Rational B-Splines (NURBS) and meshes. The key difference between them is that NURBS facilitate smooth surfaces and curves, whereas meshes approximate these formal elements via polygons and subdivisions. Projects may typically require designs to be defined in both formats, depending on the stage of the design process alongside software applications.

Above
Accurate geometrical description and curvilinear deformation, illustrated in this detailed panellization screenshot by Zaha Hadid for the Haydar Aliyev Cultural Centre, Baku.

Below
The contemporary city is increasingly viewed as a series of informational and material flows and exchanges, as investigated in the dynamic 'infrastructuralism' of the West Side Convergence project, New York, by Reiser + Umemoto.

Above and left
The seminal 'datascapes' used to illustrate MVRDV's research opened new avenues for discourse on design ideas and the nature of landscape and urbanism, as shown by their image for Waste Sector from Metacity Datatown (left). Alongside such research, the office continues to develop striking projects such as the Sky Village proposal for Rødovre (above).

Bottom left and below
The organic geometry of the bays for FOA's International Airport in Shenzhen was inspired by woven bamboo, sea ripples and the floating ribbons in traditional Chinese dance, coupled with highly pragmatic responses to the effect of the sun on the building. The resulting asymmetrical roof system is set in relation to sun-path and shading parameters, whilst also providing skylights.

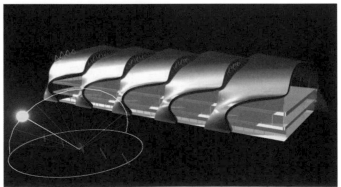

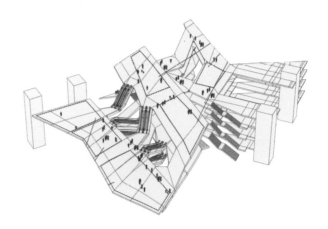

Top left, above and left
This geometry study for the Taipei Performing Arts Centre by EMERGENT/Tom Wiscombe was developed in CAD to enable circulation, structure and programme to be evolved in an integrative manner.

Bottom
In these CAD images for Neri Oxman's Raycounting project, the designer explored a novel method for developing form through light-ray orientation and intensity. By assigning light parameters to flat planes, 3D double-curvature surfaces are produced that are subsequently translated using digital fabrication techniques into physical objects.

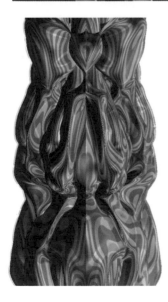

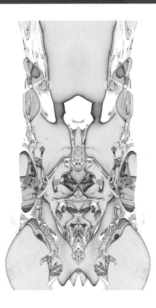

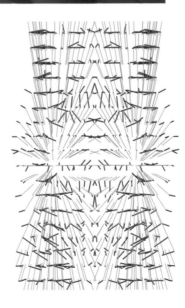

STEP BY STEP ADVANCED COMPUTATIONAL DESIGN

The design development of many contemporary projects requires designers to engage with a variety of digital tools to explore the implications of their ideas and generate appropriate data for the manufacture and assembly of the building. In this example, a range of analytical and design software is used to allow the architect to thoroughly test and understand their creative ideas from concept to fabrication.

The House in Dublin project by Amanda Levete Architects (AL_A) uses daylight to dramatically animate a deep plan. This is achieved through the careful articulation of a curved roof-shell surface, perforated with glazed elements. The plan is penetrated by a central courtyard, providing high levels of daylight and natural ventilation to all internal spaces, and a discreet external private space that also receives sunlight.

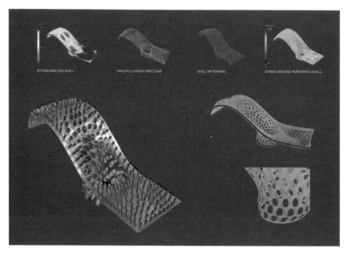

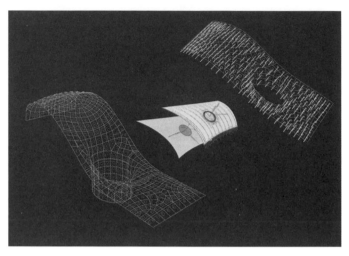

1 Volumetric studies use a series of physical models to examine the design's curvilinear geometry. Given the complexity of the form, these are a product of digital fabrication themselves – using 3D printing and contouring for accuracy so as to explore more refined aesthetic decisions.

2 Surface-stress analysis is carried out on the proposed curved roof-shell structure to check for stability and areas of high stress. The continuous skin functions as a funnel for the collection of rainwater, so additional 'live' loads are added to test their implications.

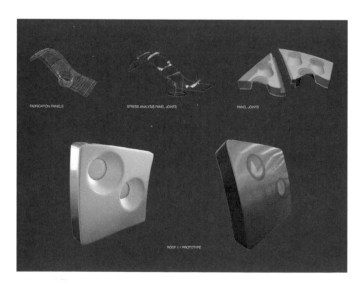

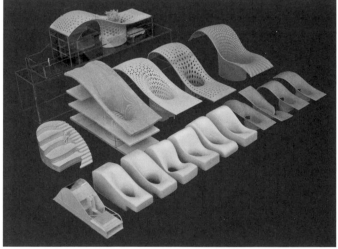

3 Once the curvilinear form is sufficiently developed, patterning parameters are applied to the skin, as the composite roof panels will be manufactured off site and installed in large sections.

4 This then enables individual panels to be determined, a number of which are fabricated as digital, then 1:1 physical, prototypes. This allows the design team to conduct further tests on detail components, such as structural and thermal integrity, as well as to explore more refined aesthetic decisions.

A photorealistic digital render
using data from analyses and
design development to give
an accurate visualization of the
proposed project.

Below
The 'rubber sheet' geometry
afforded by NURBS has been
instrumental in the design and
production of many contemporary
architectural projects. Whilst
such design tools may allow the
fabrication of curvilinear forms this
is not always the case, as shown
in these design-development
screenshots for ONL's iWeb
project in which the NURBS are
used to generate specific planar
components in relation to each
other. (Compare these images
with the final design on page 13.)

Below
The 'rubber sheet' geometry
afforded by NURBS has been
instrumental in the design and
production of many contemporary
architectural projects. Whilst
such design tools may allow the
fabrication of curvilinear forms this
is not always the case, as shown
in these design-development
screenshots for ONL's iWeb
project in which the NURBS are
used to generate specific planar
components in relation to each
other. (Compare these images
with the final design on page 13.)

Bottom right
UNStudio's floating and multidirectional space for the Burnham
Pavilion in Chicago is a direct
result of its curvilinear geometry,
developed using NURBS to inform
the design and fabrication data.

3. NURBS

The ongoing development of digital modelling software
allows design to significantly depart from the Euclidean
geometrical limits that paralleled architectural thinking
for many centuries. Before digital technologies, curved
surfaces and forms were the product of approximations
using tangents to circular arcs and straight-line segments
that were translated from drawings to the building
site. In freeing the designer from the constraints of
Cartesian space, digital modelling programs typically
use the topological geometry of continuous curves
and surfaces. Also known as 'rubber sheet' geometry,
topological geometry enables curvilinear surfaces to be
described as NURBS. The curves and surfaces produced
by NURBS provide a high degree of formal control via
'control points', 'weights' and 'knots'. Extending the
rubber-sheet analogy, it is easy to imagine how if we fixed
certain points of it, added weights to others and affected
it from other positions we would be able to see the
resultant deformations as we varied our actions. NURBS
provide the mathematical underpinning for this very
simplified description of the process, and allow the user
to develop complex geometrical designs computationally
and transfer this data using CNC machinery.

The key advantage of NURBS is their role in the
production of a wide range of geometric forms, ranging
from simple volumetric solids to extensively detailed,
complex surfaces. In addition, NURBS offer a very
efficient way of representing data by using comparatively
few steps for shape computation, which is why many

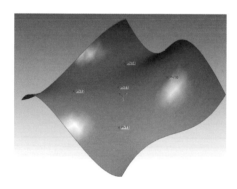

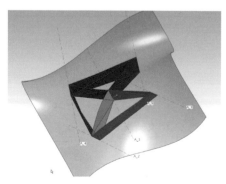

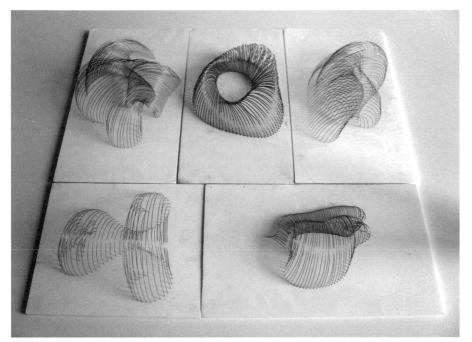

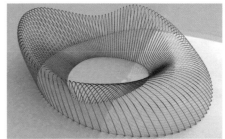

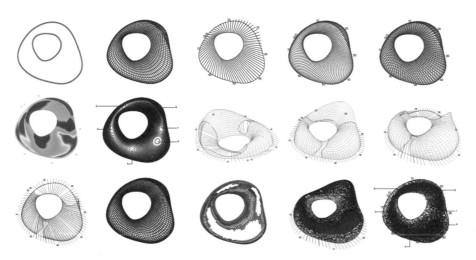

In designing a summer pavilion for the German Architecture Museum in Frankfurt am Main, Barkow Leibinger developed a series of unique radial tubes with radii that produce a circular, arched space. The initial concept stemmed from a 'slinky' toy that was explored through physical models and digital 3D modelling to refine and analyze its design variables and performance. The full-size prototype was clad with a series of polycarbonate shingles, the arrangement and shapes of which were determined by computer scripting to optimize each component within the overall system.

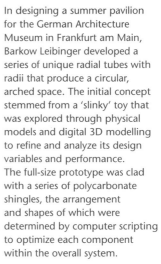

Right

The Maison Folie, Lille Wazemmes, designed by NOX provides an undulating stainless-steel skin that responds to artificial light, providing dramatic effects at night.

Below

In daytime, the scheme's form has a more solid appearance that retains its curvilinear properties but seeks to respond to the historic urban fabric of its context.

digital modelling software packages use them. If this all sounds rather abstract, then it may help to think about them as Branko Kolarevic suggests: 'NURBS are a digital equivalent of the drafting splines used to draw the complex curves in the cross-sections of ship hulls and airplane fuselages. Those splines were flexible strips made of plastic, wood or metal that would be bent to achieve a desired smooth curve, with weights attached to them in order to maintain the given shape.'[1]

1. Kolarevic, B. [ed.] (2003) *Architecture in the Digital Age: Design and Manufacturing.* Spon Press, pp.15–16.

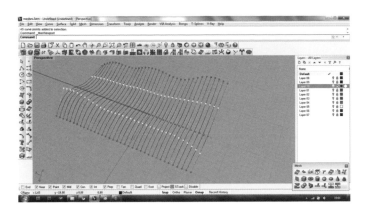
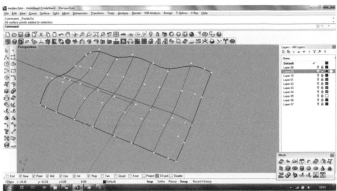

Above

NURBS can be made using a range of software programs. In this example, curves have been drawn in CAD and manipulated using their control points (left). A NURB surface is generated from the control-point curves using a 'loft' command (right).

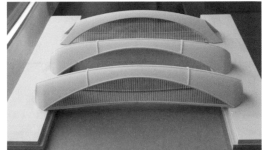

Above

In West 8's design for the Puentes Cascara Bridge, a key element of their masterplan in Madrid, the intention was to make an infrastructural element that connected to the adjacent park in terms of scale. The design was conceived as a concrete dome, from which the bridge was hung. The bridge form was explored using drawings and rapid-prototyped models to enable further refinement of the shell geometry prior to construction.

Right

The completed scheme demonstrates the smooth geometry of the concrete, which, coupled with the slim steel deck and fine cable suspension, produces a sculptural piece in keeping with the original concept.

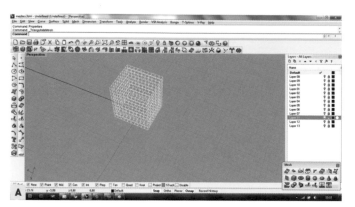

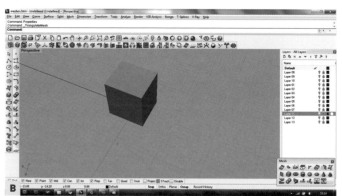

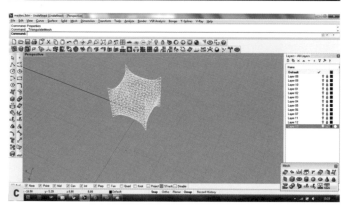

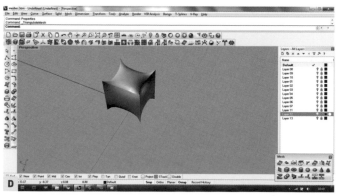

4. Meshes

The alternative method for generating this geometry is through the use of meshes. The most frequently used meshes are polygonal or polyhedral. In either case, the mesh approximates a geometric domain through an arrangement of 'vertices', 'edges' and 'faces' that combine to define the shape of the desired object. A 'vertex' is a point that describes the corners or intersections of a geometrical shape, and may also be assigned additional features such as colour and texture coordinates. An 'edge' is a connection between two vertices, whilst a 'face' is a closed set of edges describing a geometrical shape – for example, a triangle or quadrilateral – depending on the number of edges. A set of faces is known as a polygon. Polygons utilize three- or four-sided shapes because this simplifies processes such as rendering; however, more complex polygonal elements are possible if required. From a mathematical perspective a polygonal mesh may be thought of as an unstructured grid, which allows additional properties of geometry, shape and topology to be investigated through commands and manipulations. Different types of polygon meshes are used for different applications and tasks. The variety of operations performed on meshes may include Boolean logic, smoothing and simplification. Polygonal meshes are widely used in computer graphics, and consequently a significant array of algorithms exists to facilitate ray tracing, collision detection and rigid-body dynamics. Therefore, aside from rendering procedures for visualization, polygonal meshes are most commonly applied in digital modelling to develop physical simulation for Finite Element Analysis (FEA) and Computational Fluid Dynamics (CFD).

A A polygon mesh on a primitive object from software library.

B The polygon mesh rendered using a primitive mesh.

C The same primitive object having been subject to smoothing and triangulation mesh commands.

D Rendered view of the smooth mesh object. Note the difference with the image above.

STEP BY STEP WORKING WITH MESHES

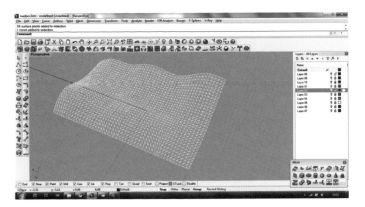

1 A basic polygon mesh is triangulated using the software's transformation menu.

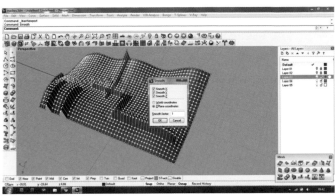

2 The control points are switched on and the mesh is manipulated using these points, ready to set up the smooth-mesh operation.

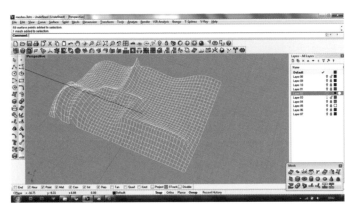

3 The resulting polygon mesh after smoothing.

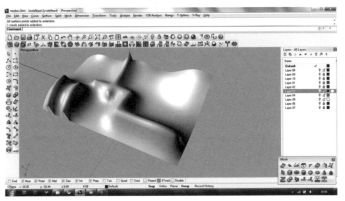

4 Rendered view of the polygon mesh following smoothing.

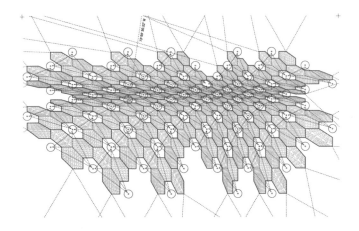

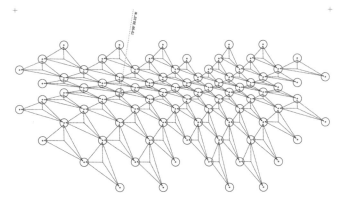

Meshes are useful digital tools for architects, especially in the design generation of complex patterns. These screenshots from the design development of Aurora by Future Cities Lab illustrate the way an overall system of panels is articulated through mesh geometry and synthesized together (left). This enables the designer to work with a network of components that, through their relative connections, may be manipulated individually whilst affecting the entire system (right).

Case study Meshes as interactive surfaces

Phillip Beesley – Hylozoic Ground, Venice, 2010.

Hylozoic Ground is an immersive, interactive environment that moves and breathes around its viewers. Part of the Hylozoic Soil series developed by architect and sculptor Philip Beesley with collaborator Rob Gorbet, an expert mechatronics engineer, this environment can 'feel' and 'care'. Next-generation artificial intelligence, synthetic biology and interactive technology create an environment that is nearly alive. The design of the components, assemblies and actuated devices of the Hylozoic series is a collaborative, evolutionary process. Design hypotheses, sketch models, experiments and tests are produced in many cycles for each component. This process incrementally refines and improves the structure in specific ways – strengthening a local weakness, preventing a joint cracking or increasing range of motion. Initial production tends to focus on the component itself, clarifying and refining its individual qualities. Interface between an individual component and other devices is addressed in further cycles. Understanding how a component functions in its larger context – at the level of the assemblies, actuated devices or integrated systems of which it is part, and of the environment as a whole – is fundamental to individual component design.

A, B AND C Acrylic, copolyester and silicone – resilient, flexible, self-supporting materials – are used to manufacture components in the environments. The most commonly used material is sign-grade impact resistant (IR) acrylic. Resistant to distributed bending stress, IR acrylic is free of 'grain' or directionally biased stiffness. IR acrylic is used for the chevrons that comprise the Hylozoic diagrid meshwork and the 'skeletons' of most Hylozoic assemblies and devices. The transparency of the hard IR acrylic is preserved by the particular laser-cutting process used in the studio, which polishes the edges of the plastic.

A

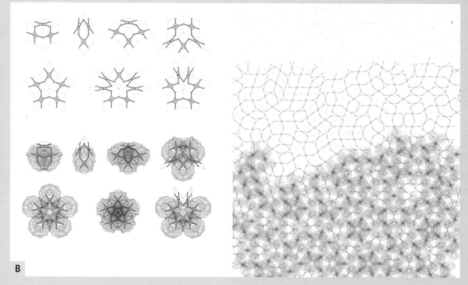

B

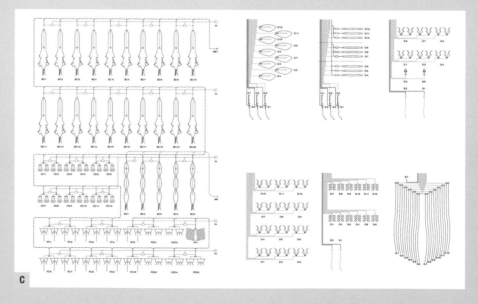

C

D Localized, or point, stress can cause cracking and failure in the acrylic. To take advantage of its strengths and prevent weaknesses, a number of features have been developed including snap-fit joints, crack-stop corners and gussets. Copolyester is more flexible than IR acrylic, with increased resistance to cracking and corner stresses but at the cost of a somewhat cloudy appearance. These qualities make it suitable for hinges and flexible ribbons, seen in the 'tongue' cores of the sensor lashes and breathing pores.

E Specialized snap-fit acrylic joints are predominantly used for joining mechanisms required by the Hylozoic meshwork, assemblies and devices. Snap-fit joints are common in industrial and product design, where they appear in such forms as the lip of a felt-tip pen or the snaps on vacuum-formed retail packaging. A standardized joint recurs within the system. The joint, which has undergone many iterations and stages of refinement, connects two laser-cut acrylic components axially, tangentially or in parallel. IR acrylic has proven effective and reliable for manufacturing snap-fit joints, and requires no other mechanical fasteners or adhesives. The length and thickness of the 'jaws' and size of the ridges can be varied to produce loose, temporary connections or tougher, more permanent joints. While the flexibility and hardness of IR acrylic make it an excellent choice for snap-fit joints and bendable hinges, the flexural stresses on the material tend to concentrate at sharp corners, leading to cracking and failure. 'Crack-stop' detailing involves filleting or rounding the interior angles to distribute stress over a greater area. The amount of filleting or easing required is often fairly small relative to the size of the component. In some cases, the easing can be pushed into an internal cavity in the component. This approach is often used when a part's U-shaped 'crotch' needs to provide a positive stop to secure and limit the movement of another part. Crack-stop corner detailing is employed in a variety of components, including latching clips employed to secure air muscles in 'swallowing' columns, tightly fitted voids for modular jacks in actuated devices and buckle fasteners for securing whisker sensors.

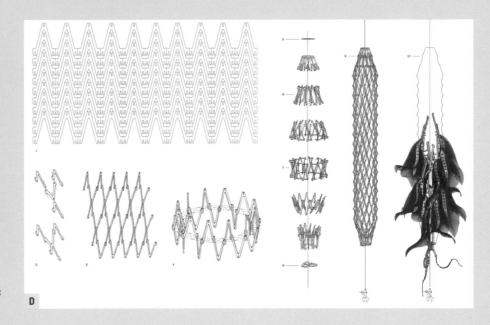

D

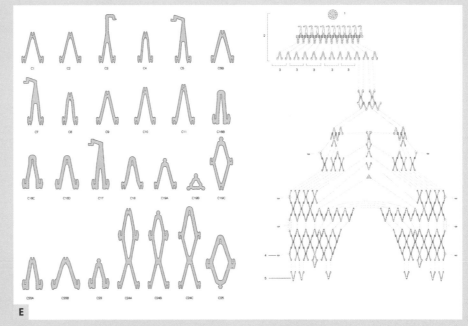

E

The manufacturing stage is fundamental to the advancement of component design. Arrayed components are reconciled with the rectangular dimensions of a sheet of IR acrylic, scaled to fit the bed of a CNC laser cutter. The organization of the array prior to cutting can add another variable to component design, especially for components that will be produced in greater numbers. In order to use materials efficiently and reduce waste, the shape of the component is refined so that it fits as tightly as possible with duplicates and other components on the same sheet. In the case of the chevrons comprising the expansive mesh lattice, the tessellation of the component has been refined to the point where they are fully nested and share edges. This makes it possible to remove overlapping lines, greatly reducing cutting time and virtually eliminating material waste. IR acrylic responds well to laser cutting, which produces smooth, clear edges. The laser's heat tends to vaporize the upper surface more than the lower, creating V-shaped cuts and bevelled edges. The greater the thickness of acrylic, the more power is required to cut through the material – resulting in more pronounced sloping of the cut edges. Tuning both snap-fit and simpler, slotted joints becomes increasingly difficult in components cut from the thickest acrylic, since the diameter of a slot at its upper edge may be significantly wider than that at the lower. Given this eccentricity of laser-cut pieces, thinner IR acrylic stock material is selected wherever possible; this has the added benefit of reducing weight and cutting time.

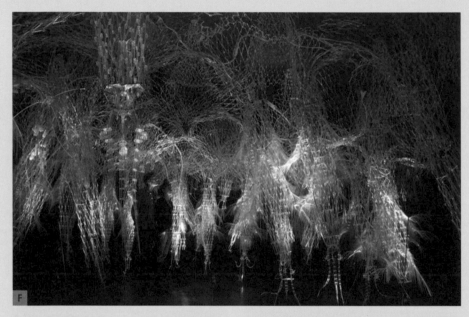

F, G AND H The interactive geotextile mesh 'senses' people in proximity to it and responds with peristaltic wave movements, appearing to 'breathe' around its occupants.

5. Curvilinear formations

One of the most important features of digital design is in its capacity to develop complex curvilinear geometries, a relatively difficult feat using traditional design and construction processes. The early novelty of these formal gestures quickly exploded into a style sometimes referred to as 'BLObitecture', derived from the Binary Large Object feature in the software that enabled such designs. However, architects generally appear to have relaxed their fascination with this approach in recent times and absorbed these geometries into more subtle and sophisticated design proposals. The reason for this surge in popularity was that prior to the development of CAD and CAM technologies, curved surfaces and forms were very difficult to design and fabricate. As they suddenly became realizable this led to an experimentation with tectonics that continues today, as architects explore the nature of façades as fluid skins and building programmes as curvilinear organizations and spatial flows. The widely published, and often iconic, projects that make extensive use of curvilinear geometry have unquestionably led to further innovation and investigation, but there has also been a residual occurrence that belies this movement. The complexity of curvilinear formations has meant that numerous architects have returned to being highly engaged in the fabrication process to ensure the design intent is carried through into the making. As a consequence of this involvement, designers have inherited greater control of the construction process since the digital design data is so closely integrated with digital manufacturing technologies. Such shifts in the design process are clearly advantageous, as they permit the designer to participate more fully than ever before through a seamless digital workflow in which design information is also construction information. This direct correlation between design and fabrication has fuelled a wealth of complex forms and structures, whose articulation and material expression challenges existing architectural conceptions. However, rather than being an end in itself the computational capacity to handle and work with these geometries has provided an expanded platform across which digital design tools may explore the boundaries of tectonics and aesthetics – either through simple, formal inquiry or relational systems that may generate their own designs.

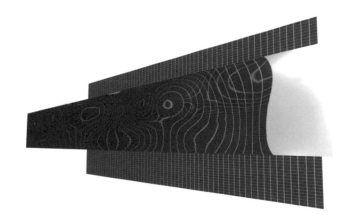

For the Home Couture project in Berlin, Franken Architekten developed a visual-kinetic installation, the *Liquid Wall*. Using a computer simulation to affect an acrylic-glass pane with a vibration 'caused' by the passer-by's gaze, the wall is distorted, making the interior oscillate. The integrated digital design and fabrication process enables the production of non-standard tiles for the façade.

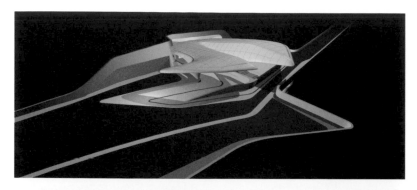

Left and below left
Zaha Hadid's groundbreaking design for the Nordpark Cable Railway, Innsbruck, comprises four stations which each respond to specific site conditions whilst connecting through a cohesive formal language of fluidity. Each station contains two primary contrasting elements, the 'shell' of the lightweight organic roof of double-curvature glass, which appears to float above the 'shadow' of a concrete plinth. The resultant artificial landscape communicates movement and circulation within the railway system. Digital fabrication techniques, primarily CNC milling and thermoforming, facilitated an accurate and automatic translation of the computer-generated design into the built structures.

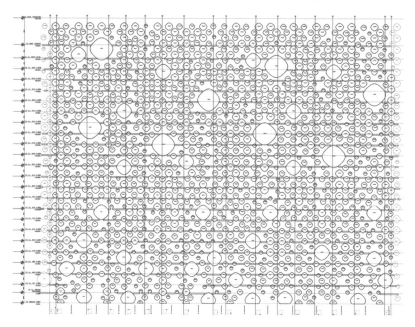

Above and right
The construction process of the O-14 Tower in Dubai, by Reiser + Umemoto, uses a concrete shell to provide an efficient structural 'exoskeleton', freeing the core from the usual high-rise structural loads and offering column-free interiors. The rolled-out shell illustrated here is organized as a diagrid, optimized by a system of continuously varying apertures providing the necessary structural support whilst efficiently localizing material where it is required. This efficiency and modulation allows the shell to create a wide range of atmospheric and visual effects in the tower without altering basic structural form, thus affording systematic analysis and construction. As a result, the tower's pattern design combines a capillary branching field, gradients of vertical articulation, opacity, environmental effects and structural and turbulence fields.

The HtwoOexpo pavilion, Neeltje Jans Island, designed by NOX, is a prototypical building showcasing a new language of form, utilizing continuous geometry to allow walls to flow from floors and in turn become ceilings. The pavilion was also the first of its kind to fully integrate new media to enhance visitors' experience and the spatial characteristics.

Right and below
The curvilinear geometry of the overall form arises from a non-standard steel frame of curved ribs and straight beams, as shown in the construction photo and plan.

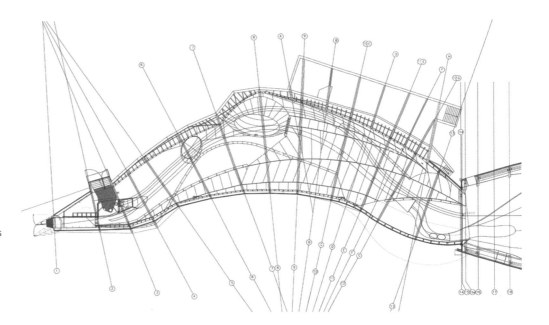

Left
The pavilion's external envelope was designed using similar technology to that found in aeronautics and shipbuilding, developing a smooth monocoque skin and thereby providing cohesion to the form's appearance.

Above
Internal space is fluid and non-linear throughout, echoing the aquatic theme accentuated by an exhibition based on water technologies – including artificial rainfall, the spraying of mist and an ice wall – which, in conjunction with interactive electronics, enable visitors to completely change the sound, light and atmosphere of the interior.

Case study Digital making of an installation

Franken Architekten – Take Off, Terminal 2, Munich Airport, 2001.

As advertising for Munich Airport's new Terminal II, Franken Architekten created a combination of brand communication and art object with visual and kinetic interactivity, using an optical illusion.

A, B AND C Concept model illustrating the principle behind the lenticular image: visual information 'changing' in relation to movement.

D, E, F AND G A parametric, digital node model was developed using Autodesk MAYA 'cloth' tool.

H The forces generating its shape were inscribed in the object and the viewer can sense their impact on the form.

I View of the final installation.

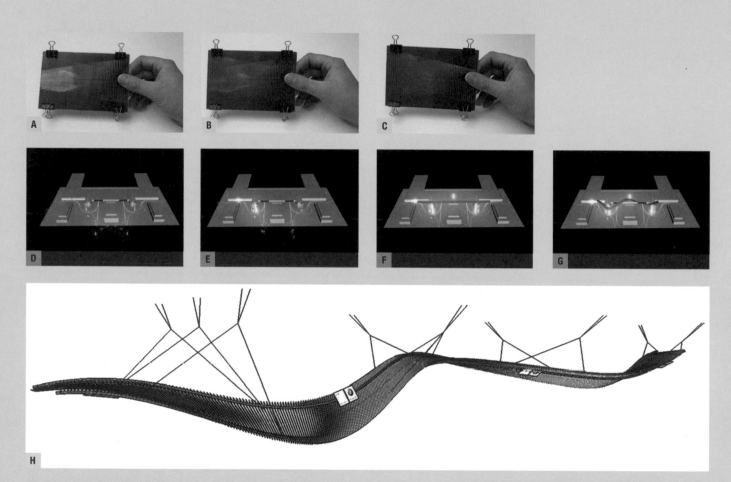

Case study Weaving walls through space

Gramazio & Kohler ETH Zurich – Structural Oscillations, Venice, 2007–8.

A

For their contribution to the 11th Venice Architectural Biennale, Gramazio & Kohler ETH Zurich conceived a 100m-long brick wall flowing as a continuous ribbon through the Swiss Pavilion.

A To achieve this the wall's design was conceived as a system with open parameters. The course of a single, continuous curve carried all the generative information necessary to determine the design.

B This curve functioned as a conceptual interface that negotiated the needs of the exhibited groups. As each group's requirements were modified, the three-dimensional, undulating wall could be automatically regenerated.

C The wall design followed algorithmic rules, and its complex shape was determined by the constructive requirement that each single, 4m-long segment stand firmly on its own. Where the course of the generative curve was almost straight, meaning that elements could possibly be tipped over by visitors, the wall's footprint began to swing, increasing its stability.

D Through its materiality and spatial configuration the completed wall, consisting of 14,961 individually rotated bricks, enters into a direct dialogue with the Modernist brick structure from 1951 by Swiss architect Bruno Giacometti. This further emphasized the plastic malleability of the wall, which acquired an almost textile character in oscillating contrast to the firm materiality of the bricks.

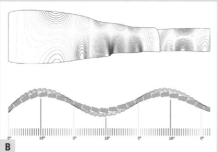

B

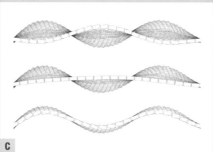

C

D

6. Parametric and generative design

Parametric design enables the designer to define relationships between elements or groups of elements, and to assign values or expressions to organize and control those definitions. It is usually applied within a three-dimensional CAD program. However, unlike the limitations raised earlier as a result of the independent nature of elements in the design, the underlying principle here is of connectivity and relationship. Parametric design addresses the constraints of traditional CAD operations by supplanting the designer's direct interaction with the design elements – adding, subtracting, copying, etc. – with the development of a series of relationships by which elements connect and build up the design. The designer may, at any time, alter the values or equations that form the relationships between elements and the effects of these changes will be incorporated into the system, which reflects them visually. On this latter point, it should be stressed that not all developments will result in a perceptible, i.e. visual, change to the design. The relationships are subsequently edited as the designer observes the effects of the revisions, as the connected system of elements evolves and the desired results are chosen based on relevant 'performative' and aesthetic criteria. In addition, complex assemblies of elements may be grouped or 'collapsed' together to form a new, customized element defined by the designer. This process may undergo further iterations, allowing the designer to develop bespoke variations that may be used in future projects. Although often perceived as a relatively recent development, parametric design was actually one of the early concepts in CAD. Ivan Sutherland's 1963 PhD thesis, *Sketchpad: A Man-machine Graphical Communications System*, proposed the first graphical user interface to enable a designer to draw on the computer and effect changes to the design parametrically. Despite the technology of the period limiting the full potential of this system, Sutherland foresaw the advantages of this type of interface: 'A display connected to a digital computer gives us a chance to gain familiarity with concepts not realizable in the physical world. It is a looking glass into a mathematical wonderland.'[2]

As with any design tool, there are positive and negative aspects to parametric design. The primary advantage is twofold: once the relationships have been established the system may run autonomously within its parameters and explore novel solutions that may not be apparent to the designer; and, as the design is always kept consistent with these parameters, the designer has greater opportunity to explore them without time-consuming reworkings. However, it is in the very task of establishing all the relationships within the parametric system that the main disadvantage is to be found. The parametric-design process is initially very time-consuming, particularly for the inexperienced, but perhaps an even greater challenge is the shift in mindset

2. Sutherland, I. E. (1965) 'The Ultimate Display', *Proceedings of IFIPS Congress 1965*, New York, May 1965, Vol. 2, pp. 506–508.

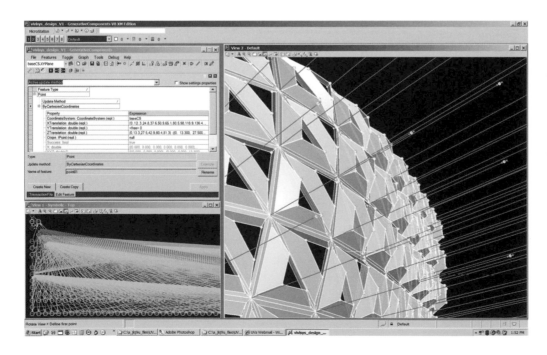

Future Cities Lab's *Vivisys* installation is an experimental double-curved acrylic-lattice vault that responds to interactions within its environment. To achieve the complex geometry, the initial surfaces were parametrically modelled using GenerativeComponents software whilst the later files for fabrication were generated using Rhino.

it requires, as Robert Woodbury explains in *Elements of Parametric Design*: 'Parametric design depends on defining relationships and the willingness (and ability) of the designer to consider the relationship-definition phase as an integral part of the broader design process ... This process of relationship creation requires a formal notation and introduces additional concepts that have not previously been considered as part of "design thinking".'[3] This is, of course, potentially exciting and rich territory, as parametric design and this attendant change in the user's behaviour may further the design possibilities by enabling ideas to be developed in an explicit, effective manner – thereby contributing to an understanding of the process and improving methods of its communication.

Let us therefore consider what a parameter is. It is a quantity that is constant in a specific scenario but may vary in other situations. Whilst sometimes seen as a limit or constraint, a parameter is neither of these but does possess a value. In basic design projects there would be negligible benefit in using a parametric system, since it would not be very time-efficient. However, where a situation has complexity, and thus many different parameters, this type of design generation is extremely useful as the practitioner is able to integrate all the different aspects into one large database and manipulate it accordingly. The latter issue, concerning the generative properties of this approach, is important since one of the key features of parametric design is the ability to describe the design as a series of relationships that may be used to iterate further versions. Here we see a principal distinction between physical modelmaking, or even traditional CAD software, and using a parametric design program. In the first two modes of inquiry, every different permutation requires a new model, whether physical or digital, to be made – or at least the original one to be extensively modified through disassembly, editing and reconfiguration. By contrast, parametric design allows multiple options to be generated within values specified by the designer. That is not to imply that one approach is more successful than another, but clearly the time and effort in the first two methods is invested in the making of the designs themselves whereas, by contrast, in the latter, generative approach the designer directs time and effort into making the system that will subsequently reiterate the designs. This phenomenon is what Mark Burry refers to as 'designing the design'.[4] To understand this way of thinking and designing it is helpful to consider algorithms for architectural design in broader sense.

3. Woodbury, R. (2010) *Elements of Parametric Design*. Routledge, p.24.

4. Burry, M. (2003) 'Between Intuition and Process: Parametric Design and Rapid Prototyping' in Kolarevic, B. [ed.] *Architecture in the Digital Age: Design and Manufacturing*. Spon Press, pp.147–62.

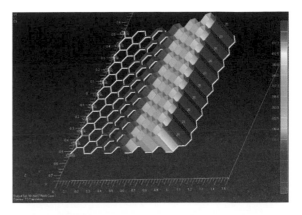

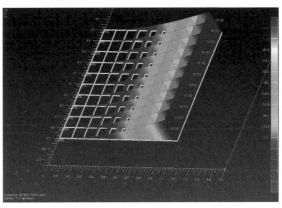

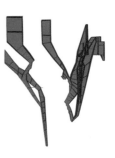

The design development of Dragonfly by EMERGENT/Tom Wiscombe in collaboration with Buro Happold necessitated the use of generative design software to explore the honeycomb patterns analogous to those found in dragonflies' wings. These patterns demonstrate rule-based interaction in relation to cell shape, depth and density, and were investigated and optimized in response to these parameters (top and middle) and pattern configuration as illustrated in the Voronoi tiling distribution (above).

Case study Parametric urban design

Zaha Hadid Architects – One North Masterplan, Singapore, 2001–21.

A

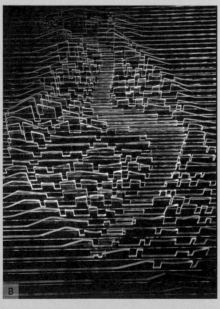

B

This masterplan echoes a consistent theme within the designs of Zaha Hadid Architects for over two decades: developing an urban architecture that uses the spatial repertoire and morphology of natural landscape formations to offer rich territory for public programming, identity and flexibility. The proposed morphology is envisaged as a system that accommodates variation whilst retaining a strong formal coherence throughout. The gently undulating overall form accommodates a wide range of built volumes and public realm, in tandem with infrastructure and connective tissue with neighbouring urban districts. Rather than using strictly Platonic geometry, the design was developed parametrically as a free, curvilinear and malleable series of deformations, pliant yet resilient to the variety of forces and flows that occur across a city district.

A The original concept painting illustrates the masterplan's dynamic, free-form geometry.

B A design-development model, laser-cut from acrylic glass to investigate the urban system as a series of landscape outlines.

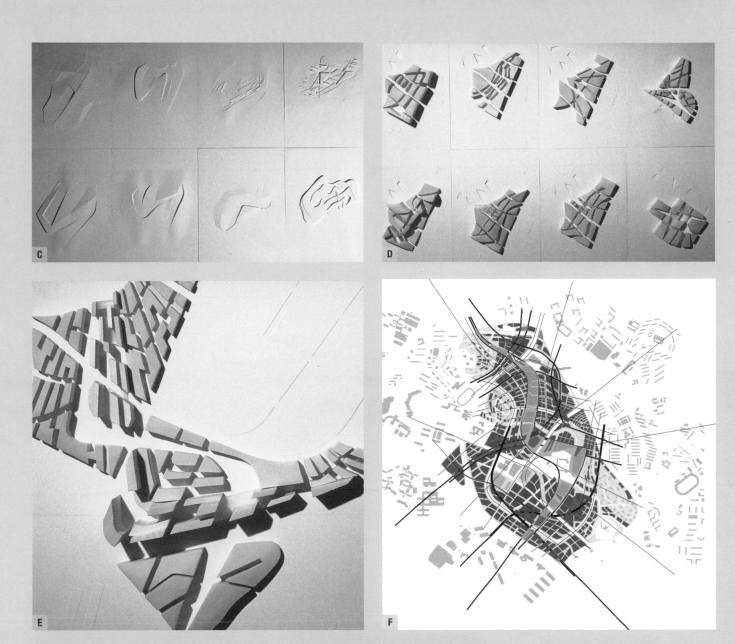

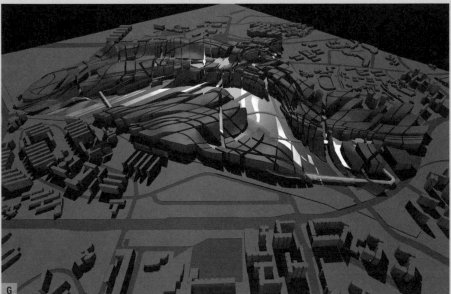

C, D, E and F The emergence of the design as urban formation through a series of physical study models (left) illustrates the project's gradual development until such a point that the design is consolidated as mirrored in the final diagram for the urban fabric (right).

G The conceptual mass/form, as developed for implementation following an intensive process of design optimization and generative development using parametric software.

Case study Parametric design of 1:1 structure

EMERGENT/Tom Wiscombe – Dragonfly, SCI-Arc, Los Angeles, 2007.

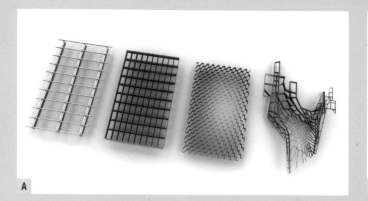

A

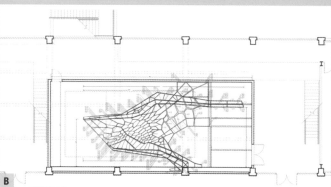

B

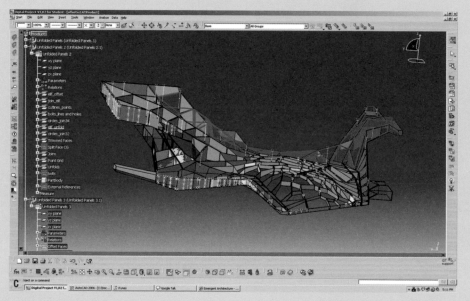

C

A The geometrical evolution of the project from a trabeated structure, via a two-way plate and then honeycomb plate to the dragonfly composite. This development achieves an emerging structural hierarchy with localized in-plane stiffness owing to the quad cells, localized flexible infill via the honeycomb cells and the adaptive response to indeterminate force flow.

B The dragonfly geometry scaled to the plan of the exhibition space. The cell size and density of the design are controlled by the boundary condition, the 'veins' taking on complex shapes in relation to force flow.

C Screenshot from Digital Project software, illustrating the design in a parametric scenario wherein the model may be manipulated and the resultant effects observed across the entire design.

The concept of the dragonfly wing, unique in its structural performance and exquisite formal variation, informed this installation. Nature offered a rich precedent for biomimetic design – in terms of formal and behavioural features rather than merely aesthetic considerations. In contrast to the wings found in nature – which respond to aerodynamics, lightness and mechanical functions – this installation was determined in relation to parameters including gravity, specific support points and flat material properties. The designer was keen to view the project within a broader context of research into cellularity in architecture as a departure from its pure form toward a tectonic based on emerging structural hierarchies within cellular aggregations.

In collaboration with Buro Happold, 'populations' of random structural mutations were generated and fitness-tested based on the given support and loading data. These conditions were then run through a feedback loop comprising multiple generations, and the geometry evolved toward performance criteria and novel variation. Formal coherence was balanced with structural legibility in the choice of mutations.

The fabrication techniques for the installation reflect the adaptive model produced during the design process. Firstly, a CATIA model was generated to parametrically connect hundreds of two-dimensional unfolded bands to 'live' three-dimensional geometry. Through the evolutionary nature of the design plus the addition of engineering data such as scoring, bending and drilling, the information related to these bands was automatically updated via the 'live' model. A nesting algorithm enabled the

bands to be distributed on to standard 100mm x 200mm aluminium sheets so as to reduce waste material. The sheets were inscribed and cut using CNC milling machines. The embedding into the bands of assembly data for the installation structure, including relative cell position and bending angles, ensures that the construction of *Dragonfly* is a bottom-up process without the need for conventional documentation.

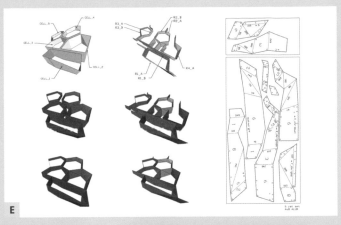

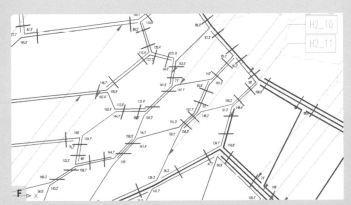

D Von-Mises analysis, illustrating equivalent
stress across the arrangement of cells.

E Development of cell connections as
bespoke elements within the structure.

F Detailed view of the parametric model, showing
cell positions, connection points and bending angles.

G This information is used to assemble the physical
installation. Reference data is clearly inscribed on
the cut components for those constructing it.

H The final installation, seemingly defying
gravity through its innovative structure
and evolutionary geometry.

7. Algorithmic architecture

Generative and parametric designs typically use graphic interfaces that retain some familiarity with conventional CAD software systems, even if they significantly extend the computer's capacity to inform the design process. Considering algorithms and their use as a medium through which we may generate and develop architectural design ideas, we need to understand that this requires an elemental shift in the way we use computers. The role of the computer in architectural design has essentially bifurcated. For the majority of practitioners, computers are advanced tools that allow production of complex forms and high-quality visualizations. In this scenario, the computer is an interface that enhances traditional modes of inquiry, and thus augments a designer's toolkit during the design process. However, an alternative route is gradually emerging – used by a significant number of

designers. Rather than viewing the computer merely as an interface, they engage with its inner workings through programming in order to further exploit its capabilities. In his authoritative book, *Algorithmic Architecture*, Kostas Terzidis convincingly argues for a total rethink in the way we approach computers. He explains the fundamental difference between these two modes of operating with computers as follows: 'Computerization is about automation, mechanization, digitization, and conversion. Generally, it involves the digitization of entities or processes that are preconceived, predetermined, and well defined. In contrast, computation is about the exploration of the indeterminate, vague, unclear, and often ill-defined processes; because of its exploratory nature, computation aims at emulating or extending the human intellect. It is about rationalization, reasoning,

Rogers Stirk Harbour + Partners' design for the Santa Maria del Pianto metro station, Naples, uses an evolutionary algorithm to develop the roof canopy. A bespoke plug-in for the Rhino software was developed by Fred Labbe of Expedition Engineering in order to map the lattice pattern of the canopy to give optimum light, shade and structural strength. The final pattern was then mapped on to a toroid shape that will be fabricated using vertically aligned steel plated together to form the canopy's lattice. The image to the right illustrates the progress of the evolutionary algorithm, whilst those below and below right show a structural-stress diagram and visualization of the design.

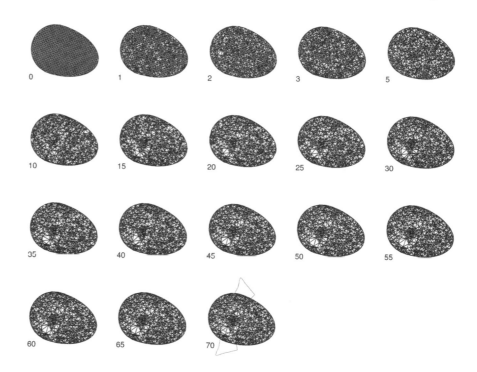

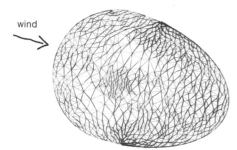

logic, algorithm, deduction, induction, extrapolation, exploration, and estimation. In its manifold implications, it involves problem solving, mental structures, cognition, simulation, and rule-based intelligence, to name a few.'[5]

By comprehending the distinction between these terms, it is possible to view the typical use of computers as involving processes of computerization rather than computation. In computerization, the ideas already exist in the mind of the designer and are translated into digital data through the computer's software interface. Whilst there is evidently the possibility to effect change upon these ideas, such transformations are constrained by the options and processing capacities (or 'rules') of the software program being used. In contrast, algorithmic architecture utilizes a 'scripting language' to enable the designer to directly access the computational ability of the computer. Indeed, algorithms communicate the creative intentions of the designer to the computer by acting as a mediator between the two. Whilst this potentially suggests a very empowering method of working, there are two primary factors to consider. The first one relates to the 'process' of an algorithm, which must be specified in a gradational manner in order to build its logic effectively. The second issue concerns the required accuracy of an algorithm since one simple error, such as an incorrect character, will typically result in it being unable to work, or 'run', properly – if at all. These two features of working with algorithms highlight a difference required in the designer's mindset and practice, since architects usually design objects with contingencies and adaptive flexibility rather than with extreme precision. As such, novice designers will often find using algorithms and scripting languages time-consuming and difficult to begin with, but perseverance will reap the benefits of this approach. It is perhaps therefore unsurprising that the algorithms in most CAD software usually process command tasks 'invisibly' in the background. Parametric software systems often act as a bridge between the two extents of this situation as they localize algorithms within a visually orientated graphic interface rather than through exposure to the scripting language.

Algorithms were traditionally used as tools to help solve mathematical problems. In 1936, Alan Turing was responsible for a major technological breakthrough when he invented the Turing Machine, a general-purpose computational device that gave a framework for the definition of an algorithm, which, as Paul Coates has noted, 'defined computation at such an abstract level that it could be applied to the widest range of problems.'[6] Through his innovative work, Turing became the forebear of artificial intelligence and the notion that computers

The application of algorithmic design software for the Central Embassy in Bangkok by AL_A allowed a high level of visual complexity across the building's envelope through the interaction of three-dimensional tiles across the large surface area.

5. Terzidis, K. (2006) *Algorithmic Architecture*. Architectural Press, p.xi.

6. Coates, P. (2010) *Programming.Architecture*. Routledge, p.53.

could not only be used as tools in themselves but might also enable new thinking about knowledge. Algorithmic architecture uses the processing power of the computer to directly address a design problem by searching strategically through possible solutions. This search, unlike the 'creative leaps' that occur to a designer using conventional modes of inquiry, is characterized by a number of rational, consistent and finite steps. Therefore, providing the problem can be defined in logical terms a solution can be found to it. This, however, reveals only one of the ways in which algorithms may be used, since it actually replicates traditional design methods. In addition to this approach, algorithms may operate parallel processes to those of the designer and thus provide design tools that generate novel concepts and speculative forms, which in turn further influence the designer. Mark Burry reinforces this position observing that 'scripting can also be the antidote to standardisation forced by an ambition to lower production costs, rather than any more sophisticated motivation: the previously elusive opportunities for multiple versioning and bespoke production can now be considered more seriously through the use of scripting.'[7] Algorithms can also be run to explore possible solutions unknown to the designer by simulating natural processes such as genetics that may explore the evolutionary adaptation of various permutations of a design over time. By thus effecting various 'generations' of design solutions, algorithms create, evaluate and then choose the most suitable solutions and these are further developed through a process of mutation and mating similar to evolution in the natural world. This method uses the advantages of computational processing technology, i.e. speed and precision, and applies it to a form of 'natural selection', using the computer to seek out the 'best' solution as a result of a series of calculations. The use of biological paradigms to generate and evolve design ideas is an area of algorithmic design garnering considerable interest, and is typically referred to as 'morphogenesis'.

7. Burry, M. (2011) *Scripting Cultures: Architectural design.* John Wiley.

Right
The Babiy Yar – Inverted Monument project is part of Kokkugia's ongoing research into behavioral design methodologies and uses algorithms to generate a landscape with a differentiated field of intensities, which culminates in an intense aggregation of the monument.

Bottom right
The space of remembrance within the inverted monument is generated through the interaction of agent-based components. The component logic of this carved space is polyscalar: self-similar algorithmic agents operate across scales to form a continuous tectonic, creating a spectacular series of spatial affects.

STEP BY STEP ALGORITHMIC ARCHITECTURE

As part of his Green Oil Economy thesis project, John Dent used algorithms to explore the possibilities for optimizing environmental performance in relation to form for the design of a wind-turbine factory in Birkenhead. The steps illustrated here describe the development of a roof system that would respond to the sun, and was based on each individual roof component reacting to its solar angle.

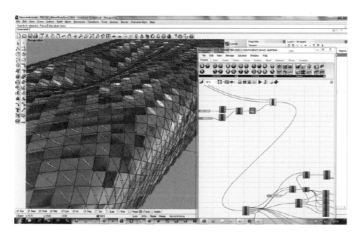

1 A 'sun system' was applied, enabling the designer to observe the effects and changes of the roof system according to time of day, month and year, with apertures opening and closing to vary internal lighting as required.

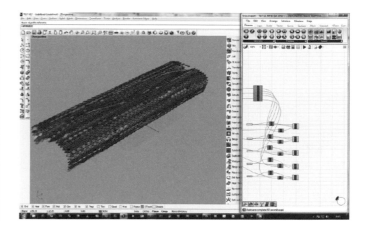

2 The result is a geometrical model and system that is dynamic and easily transformed, until such a point that the design is sufficiently determined.

3 Detailed view of roof envelope, illustrating individual tile behaviour in relation to overall composition of surface geometry.

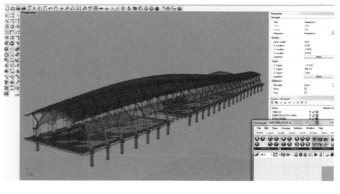

4 The final design may be fixed at any point, but even after this further changes are possible since every step of the process is 'recorded' by the software and therefore is able to be controlled again. Thus, any of the algorithmic relationships established in the system may be further nuanced and explored.

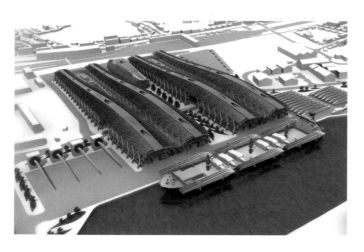

Left Digital visualization showing an aerial view of the final design in context.

Case study Algorithms as design generation

Joanna Szulda – Crafted Canopy, 2009.

A

B

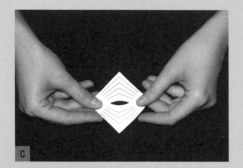

C

D

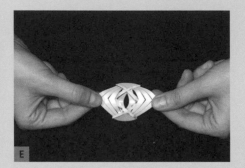

E

A, B, C, D and E The previously laser-cut paper surface is subject to a series of experimental and often improvisational manual procedures that involve folding, pressing, twisting, wrapping, etc., while preserving the continuity of the folded surface. Continuous, simultaneous unwrapping and unfolding of the crafted components allows for mapping of the process based on patterns left by the procedures on the flat form. Through this testing sequence, a 3D object emerges with the desired stiffness, rigidity and structural span.

F, G, H, I, J and K This part of the experiment focuses on visual understanding and testing of the evolution of previously crafted 3D components into various spatial combinations. After using a 3D scanner, the spatial component, now in digital form, is processed using 3D modelling software, Rhinoceros. The 3D component is now tested through further manual folding and digital modelling.

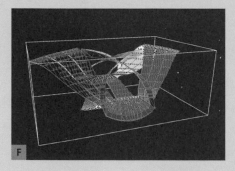

F

G

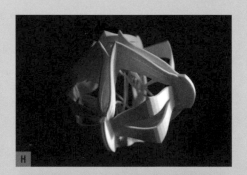

H

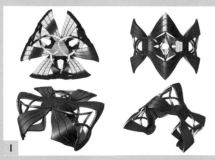

I

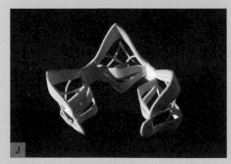

J

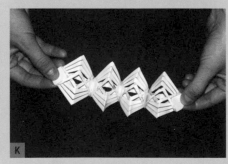

K

This research project combines analogue folding methods with digital techniques into a creative, user-responsive, multipurpose construct. The focus is on the process and evolution of a component. The language of 'paperfold' algorithms is not formal; it is a combination of geometry, baroque ornamental patterns and visual narratives. The following experiment explores the potential of paper folding for crafting an ornamental component applicable to a canopy prototype. The folding process is fundamentally experimental and morphogenetic, whereby the sequence of transformations influences the design object. The neologism 'paperfold' is used here to describe the object being in transition in the folding process.

L AND M In the subsequent transition phase, the language of algorithms forms a combination of visual narratives. The algorithms are translated into spatial volumes according to repetitive patterns creating structural and organizational 'families'. Although Algorithm I and II give a visually interesting composition, their application to create a canopy is limited, both construction- and purpose-wise. Therefore, only Algorithm III is further manipulated in the digital testing phase to create a Generative Algorithm – the prototype model of a canopy. The Generative Algorithm is an arrangement of convex strands formed of experimental Algorithm III, aligned into a curvilinear structure.

N, O AND P The prototype canopy proposal is printed out by a 3D printer using Selective Laser Sintering technology. The digital processing of the components to arrive at an SLS-printed model in a powdered material allows for a firmer construction than that made of paper. The combination of digital modelling and SLS printing also makes it possible to push the boundaries of the construction further and improves the visualization of the final construct.

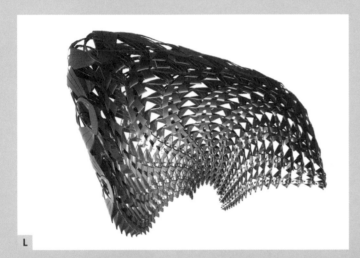

L

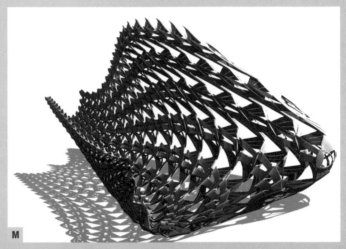

M

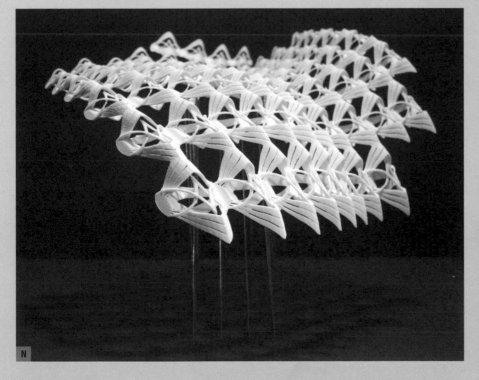

N

O

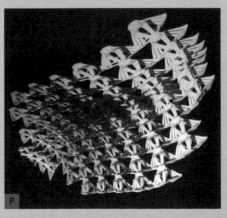

P

8. Morphogenesis

As part of his PhD thesis on novel computation for designing complex architectural morphologies, Daniel Richards developed an initial study into how performative formal behaviours undefined by typological expressions may be produced by integrated design methodologies. This series demonstrates a number of morphogenetic iterations, generated computationally, of a canopy and the permutations of its various apertures in response to daylight optimization balanced with limiting overheating.

Earlier in this section, it was explained that digital technologies, far from simply representing architectural designs have also developed as tools to generate formal ideas. The generation of digital forms is a result of a computational method highly contrasting with traditional modes of design because it uses a series of logical steps or calculations as opposed to the internal creative impetus of the human designer. Morphogenesis is the evolutionary development of form in an organism, or part thereof. Understanding that living organisms may be viewed as systems, and that these evolve their often complex forms and behavioural patterns as a result of interactions between their components over time, means that such dynamic, biological growths and transformations may also be simulated. Key to the theme of morphogenesis is the concept of 'emergence', which has gained increasing popularity in a variety of disciplines as it is related, amongst other areas, to evolutionary biology, cybernetics and complexity theory. Emergence is perhaps most easily understood as those characteristics of a system that cannot

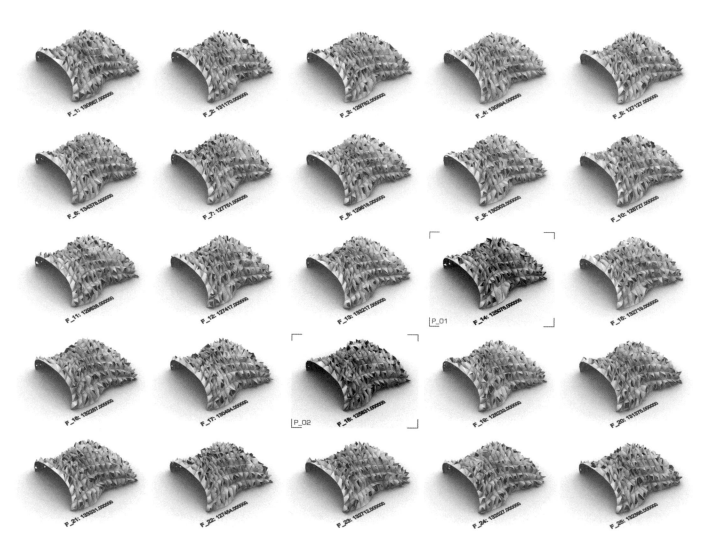

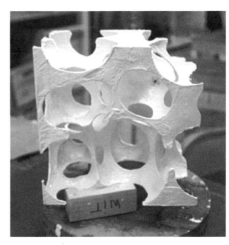

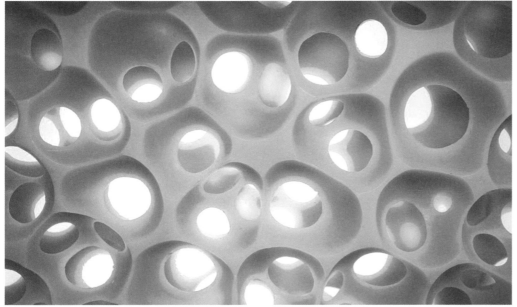

AMO is the design and research counterpart to OMA's architectural practice. The project shown here attempted to develop a new substance, nicknamed 'foam', for the Prada Epicenter store in Los Angeles. This exploration into the redefinition of surface and material was evolved as a morphogenetic process between solid and void. Initial inquiry quickly expanded through numerous texts and prototypes to explore hole sizes, levels of transparency, depths and colours. Parallel to such physical models, 3D digital modelling translated these properties and technical parameters, which led to further prototypes fabricated via CNC milling and stereolithography methods. The final product was a polyurethane cast: an optimized condition between solid and void. Shown here in detailed view and inside the store, the resultant lighting effects and spatial qualities greatly accentuate the experience of the design.

be identified from its individual components.[8] However, in the context of architectural design Michael Weinstock provides a more expansive and useful application of the term: 'Emergence is of momentous importance to architecture, demanding substantial revisions to the way in which we produce designs … Criteria for selection of the "fittest" can be developed that correspond to architectural requirements of performance, including structural integrity and "buildability".[9] Again, whilst the use of computational processes to run morphogenetic design algorithms is comparatively recent, architects have been engaged with the notion of form finding for much longer than this. Whilst it is widely held that the work of Antoni Gaudí is the first documented experimentation in this regard, many view the pioneering projects of Frei Otto as fundamental to the development of architectural design in relation to natural systems and iterative mathematics. The foundations of morphogenesis lie in the groundbreaking work of mathematician and zoologist D'Arcy Thompson, who identified variances within species whilst recognizing underlying relationships.

Emergent behaviour, therefore, is best understood as a type of self-organization in which the components of a design evolve their arrangement, and thus the overall form may also be transformed in the process. There is mutuality between these two, since form and behaviour are interdependent and coexist in order to develop dynamic, non-linear systems. These aspects are of great interest to architects, since morphogenesis can assist the emergence of speculative designs that may explore possible scenarios in relation to the variety of parts, often known as the level of 'differentiation', and the number of connections between them, also referred to as the degree of 'integration'. Although this may sound perplexing, it is reassuring to know that the majority of this emergent behaviour is actually structured and typically the result of simple, repetitive rules that interact with one another. This may be more easily understood if we observe the behaviour of an ant colony or flock of birds. In both cases, there is no hierarchical intelligence instructing the overall system – simply a series of local, neighbouring relationships that respond to each other and transmit these interactions back into the system.

Transposed to the field of architecture, morphogenesis enables designers to evolve a series of possibilities from which a selection may be made for further development. Branko Kolarevic summarizes the potential of this approach in architecture: 'The emphasis shifts from the "making of form" to the "finding of form", which various digitally-based generative techniques seem to bring about intentionally. In the realm of the form, the stable is replaced by the variable, singularity by multiplicity.'[10] Biological systems are attractive to architects since they may be applied in a multi-scalar manner, and as such extend the descriptive tools of architectural design since a system may refer to the holistic building, an integrated façade or the nano-materiality of a specific component.

8. For an excellent overview on the subject see: Johnson, S. (2001) *Emergence: The Connected Lives of Ants, Brains, Cities and Software*. Allen Lane.
9. Weinstock, M. (2004) 'Morphogenesis and the Mathematics of Emergence' in Hensel, M., Menges, A. & Weinstock, M. *Emergence: Morphogenetic Design Strategies*. John Wiley & Sons, p.17.
10. Kolarevic, B. [ed.] (2003) *Architecture in the Digital Age: Design and Manufacturing*. Spon Press, p.13.

Diagrid roof canopy developed using morphogenetic design principles. For explanation of this process see opposite page.

STEP BY STEP MORPHOGENETIC DESIGN EVOLUTION OF A SURFACE

This project, designed by Romulus Sim, calls for a substantial re-think in the consumption, production and inhabitation cultures of our urban environment. Using innovative generative design methodologies transposed to the context of the post-industrial port of Birkenhead, the project seeks to address the abandoned waterways by a combination of preserving existing dockland activities and re-programming to facilitate aquaculture waterscapes. The arrangement of the project's infrastructural elements both in the water and on land is a result of a sophisticated process of mapping programmatic data and optimizing interrelationships within the overall system. The progressive development of micro-economies in relation to tourism, culture, education, aquafarming and business offers a highly creative and multi-layered strategic approach

that is both fully implementable and innovative in design terms. The design features a highly articulated roof canopy – developed using morphogenesis – that provides a level of shelter for the hybrid programme underneath, while also enabling daylight penetration and minimizing wind loading.

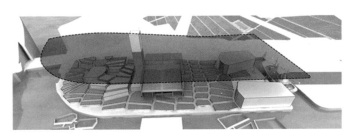

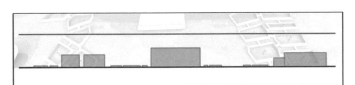

1 The canopy structure is intended as a shading device that sits over a series of objects. An appropriate datum level is set in relation to the height of the design's programme, in this case 15m.

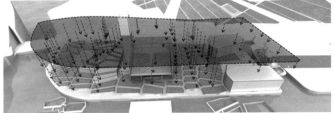

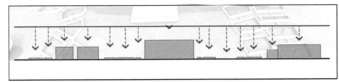

2 A data cloud is generated as a series of points, which are plotted from width-to-height ratios of each individual space, i.e. larger spans correlate to deeper roof structure, arc length and height

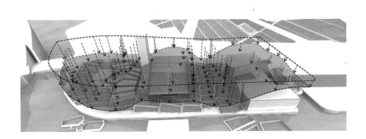

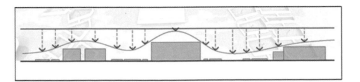

3 Using the data points, a surface is 'lofted' through them in order to generate a form that represents the canopy over the buildings below.

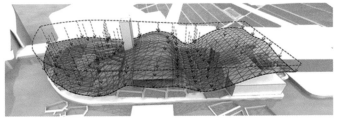

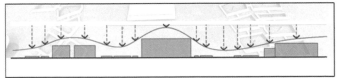

4 A diagrid structure is developed via a surface population-generation script, which controls the span of each diagrid to a maximum span of 3m in any direction.

Case study Morphogenesis and 'materialecology'

Neri Oxman – Beast, 2008–10.

Architect and designer Neri Oxman is Assistant Professor of Media Arts and Sciences at the MIT Media Lab, where she directs the Mediated Matter research group. It explores how digital design and fabrication technologies mediate between matter and environment to radically transform the design and construction of objects, buildings and systems. Oxman's goal is to enhance the relationship between the built and the natural environments by employing design principles inspired by nature and implementing them in the invention of digital design technologies. In the project Beast, she has developed a prototype for a chaise longue from a continuous surface incorporating digital form-generation protocols responsive to physical parameters. The hybrid surface, providing both structure and skin, is articulated locally to adopt thickness, pattern density, stiffness, curvature and loading capability as interdependent constraints. Numerous algorithms were generated to negotiate between the engineering and experiential aspects of the project.

A AND B A pressure-map study allocated the relative softness and hardness of the cells to cushion and support the user. The relative volume of each cell is determined by pressure data, with the overall patterning designed to increase the ratio of surface area to volume in those areas having contact with the body. Through the analysis of anatomical structures, Beast develops a balance of structural and sense data to achieve both flexibility and structural support.

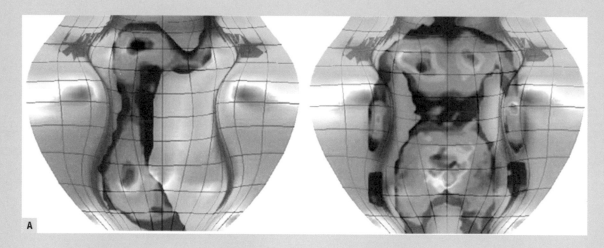

A

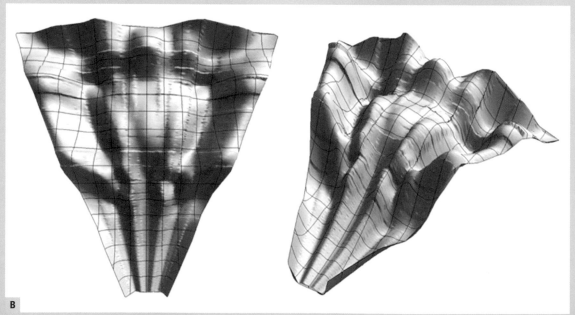

B

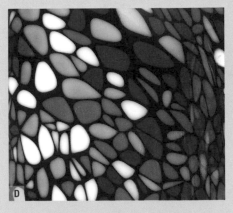

C, D AND E The cellular grain of the surface is informed by curvature values, both global and local to the object, so that smaller, denser cells are arranged in areas of steep curvature whilst larger cells are placed in areas with shallow curvature. The fabrication technique uses variable polymer composites that afford a range of physical properties. Flexible materials are positioned in surface areas under tension, with more rigid materials placed in those under compression. These surface patches are 3D-printed using an innovative multi-jet matrix technology that is capable of depositing variable materials with different properties in relation to structural and skin-pressure map data.

Case study Morphogenetic patterns as façade

Faulders Studio + Studio M – Airspace, Tokyo, 2007.

Thom Faulders was commissioned to devise a screen façade that would give the building a recognizable identity within its immediate context. In addition, it is designed to provide privacy from the street for occupants of the open-plan private residences, and buffer the weather from exterior walkways and terraces. Formally, the screen façade unifies the separated 'Living Unit' blocks on the building's top floors with the commercial spaces and landscaped areas below. The porous layers of dense vegetation surrounding the original residence influenced the conceptual direction of the screen. An anomaly amidst the concrete-and-asphalt neighborhood, this house and vegetation were subsequently razed to make way for the

new development on the site. Referencing the transitory biomorphic and atmospheric qualities of this original 4m-deep green space, a new artificial buffer zone was created – now compressed directly on to the building and only 20cm deep. To achieve this new protective atmosphere, rich in density and complexity, a layered skin system separated by an air gap was configured to wrap the building as a non-uniform porous mesh. A collaboration was established with design technologist Sean Ahlquist of Proces2 in San Francisco to develop a system for generating the patterned geometry of differentiated voids that puncture and articulate the two skins.

A Series of card prototypes exploring different patterns and surface porosity.

B The overlapping surfaces of this geometric pattern of ellipses are developed at a larger scale to examine its characteristics.

C This prototype is further augmented with edges around the apertures, and external lighting conditions evaluated.

D A radical rethink of the surface geometry ensues during the evolutionary design process, leading to experimentation with patterns that feature variable apertures.

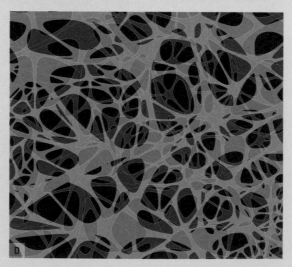

The result is a cellular environment that creates a dynamic, changing zone between public and private — where framed views shift as one moves through the spaces, rainwater is channelled away from walkways via capillary action and light is refracted along its glossy, white, metallic surfaces. The final Airspace screen system is a composite of two skins, each comprising two unique patterns that are then digitally merged. Separated from the building by a 20cm air gap, it is constructed using a rigid composite aluminium-and-plastic panel material, called Alpolic®, commonly used for exterior billboard backing and infrastructural protective coverings (such as beneath raised Tokyo freeways, for sound isolation). To make the cellular screen seemingly float upon the building as a tautly layered 'wrap', a matrix of extremely thin stainless-steel rods is threaded from top to bottom, to which the panels are affixed via custom-fabricated adjustable connectors.

E Once consolidated as a geometrical pattern, CAD software is used to wrap the surface around the building and optimize its effects in relation to scale.

F AND G The result is an enigmatic layered façade that offers sophisticated interplay between light and shadow.

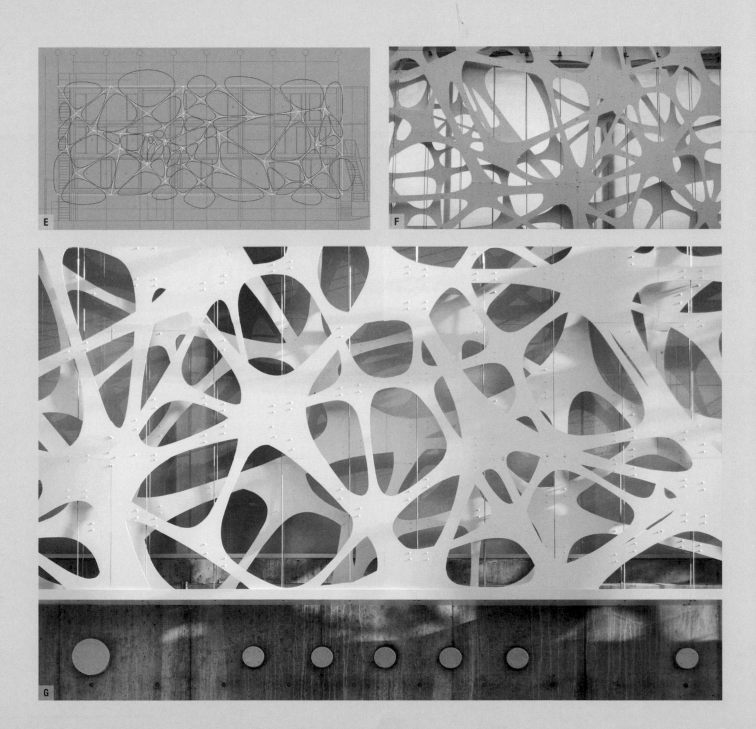

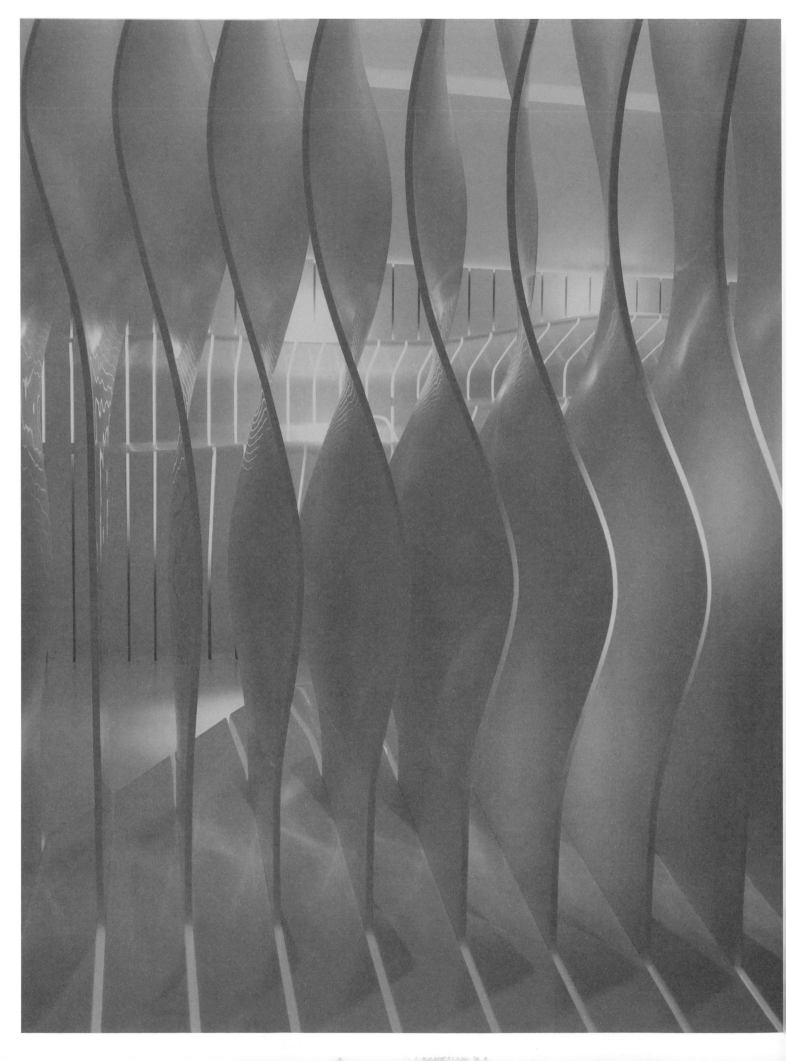

PART 2 INTEGRATION

1. Introduction

The previous section examined a number of ways in which the computer may be used as a digital design tool. It also discussed the role of computational power and its application through parametric and generative systems, algorithmic design and integration processes such as morphogenesis. Far from being a passive and inert tool, the computer is often an active and dynamic agent that not only enables the representation of creative ideas but may also generate them. The current section will build upon this knowledge, describing the range of methods for integrating creative ideas with fabrication processes at various stages of the design process, from concepts to full-scale prototypes. Furthermore, this section will reinforce the concept of architectural design as a diverse practice of making – which encourages, and is enriched by, hybrid modes of experimentation and representation, often resulting in non-linear processes of working. The advancement of architectural knowledge is fuelled by innovation and design development, and as such the modes of generation and representation in architectural design further expand the field of inquiry and discovery. Perhaps the most significant feature of the digital technologies under discussion is that the design data is often also the construction data, or very intricately connected to it, so the formal, spatial and material potential is vast.

Digital fabrication techniques also offer another characteristic that is of particular relevance here. Traditionally, the building industry's manufacturing and construction processes were only economically viable through mass production and the assembly of standard components. Digital technologies have transformed this procedure and, in a similar manner to the digital design tools described earlier, digital fabrication methods are also a generative medium through which an abundance of experimentation is available to designers. There are numerous reasons for this shift, which will be dealt with later in this section; for now, it is sufficient to know that the interdependent relationships between visualizing and making designs afford a fluid digital workflow from concept to realization. If, however, this suggests digital tools and fabrication processes as an entirely seamless system, then it is slightly misleading. As with any design tool, there are limits and tolerances of working with different digital fabrication techniques, and it is frequently through the negotiation of these constraints that designers innovate. This is particularly relevant where such techniques are combined to provide a hybridized form of production. Additionally, a vast array of material exploration suddenly opens up to the designer using digital fabrication methods – facilitating creative, efficient and highly effective uses of architectural materials. The

transformative properties of materials when translated from digital information, or indeed vice versa, emphasize the importance of engaging with generative, playful and evolutionary design as a primary architectural activity.

Of course, as with digital design tools, digital fabrication techniques may be part of a design process or completely inform it. The various degrees to which these technologies may be engaged with are often balanced between design intent and the capacities of the different methods. Indeed, the innovation that frequently arises through the use of digital fabrication must be seen in relation to the various technologies and the overcoming of their constraints rather than being stifled by them. It is important to understand that there is no prescriptive approach to digital design and fabrication; the techniques are non-linear. As we shall see, many of the limits of these techniques stem from the mindset of the designer rather than technological possibilities, so before we examine a range of digital making methods it is valuable to have a general overview of the developments that have led to their application in architecture.

Below
The degree of interaction between human and machine may vary considerably depending on the designer's approach, as shown by this image of a digitally controlled robot cutting and assembling wooden slats to an algorithmic pattern for Gramazio & Kohler's West Fest Pavilion, Wettswil am Albis, Switzerland.

Below
Michael Hansmeyer's Subdivided Column project exemplifies the creativity with which digital fabrication techniques may be applied. A column is steadily built up using 1mm-thick laser-cut paper, resulting in an extraordinarily complex three-dimensional object.

2. Hybrid techniques

Ongoing developments in digital technologies have radically altered the relationship between design idea and fabrication. Through the use of digital design, closely allied with digital making and assembly methodologies, a number of architectural projects have been wholly realized in a digital manner. This process is typically referred to as 'file-to-factory', meaning that the data from the design directly informs the technologies of making. However, this relatively closed loop of integrative design represents only one avenue of creative activity for architects, and, in both professional and educational contexts, it is worthwhile considering the use of hybrid techniques that enable designers to explore and dovetail both analogue and digital modes of inquiry as parallel and codependent activities. Crucially, this type of hybridized approach increases the instrumentality through which we may conceive, investigate and ultimately make our designs. By expanding the design toolkit with which we experiment and develop ideas, we encourage novel solutions, unexpected turns in the design process and often greater communication and comprehension of our creative impulses. In a digital age, in which the question is no longer whether a design is buildable or not, the growth areas of interest concern the best way to engage with and respond to the potential of digital fabrication. Possibly the most important development in this regard is the making of 'non-standard' components through a process of 'mass customization'.

Left and far left
By using an 'upcycling' approach to design and materials, a number of research and design projects by Greg Lynn FORM have 're-purposed' children's toys for a range of uses. The most recent, *Fountain,* made in 2010, is a functioning fountain made of large, plastic, found children's toys that have been cut and reassembled in multiple layers, with water spouting from its top and pooling at its base. Constructed from over 57 prefabricated whale and shark teeter-totters welded together, and unified with white automotive paint, the installation offers a gathering place for the warm summer months.

Left
Conceived as a series of ripples transforming space through movement, the dynamic effects of AL_A's design for Corian® Super Surfaces provide visual complexity. Advanced digital technology was used in generating the design, as well as for fabrication. AL_A also designed the making of the piece, working closely with Hasenkopf to develop a single adjustable jig that created multiple twisted surfaces from a standard flat sheet.

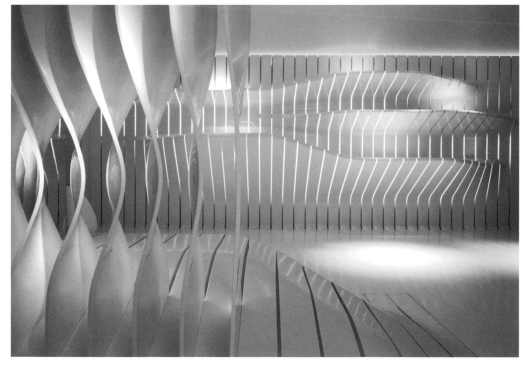

Case study Extreme integration

EMERGENT/Tom Wiscombe – Batwing, 2008.

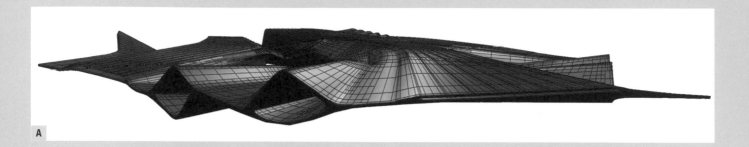

A

Batwing is part of a larger body of work creating coherent relationships between building systems through geometric and atmospheric means. The aim is to move toward a higher-order emergent 'wholeness' in architecture while still maintaining a performative discreteness of systems. The project can be understood as an articulated manifold which incorporates structural, mechanical, envelope and lighting-system behaviours. This is not to say that one of these systems is 'optimized' in terms of any functional category – the formal and ambient spatial effects of fluidity, translucency, glow and silhouette are all equally important for the overall effect. The intent is to establish a link between the sensate realm and infrastructural flows in architecture.

A The design sensibility of Batwing is driven by two types of surface transformation: the 'pleat' and the 'becoming-armature'. Pleats provide structural rigidity and direct airflow across a surface while creating a seductive ornamental patterning. The armature transforms the envelope system into a duct system, which provides supply air as well as structural continuity between envelope components.

B Deep pleats become 'air diffusers', featuring an embedded meshwork of micro-capillaries used for cooling or heating passing air. Based on the principle of water-to-air heat exchange, this system heats or cools through local radiative transfer rather than relying on 'central air'.

B

C AND D The 'language' of the piece consciously looks to automotive and aerospace design in terms of fluidity, integration of systems, and processes of construction. These disciplines have flourished through the feedback of design sensibility and extreme shaping environments, a process which has further informed the practice's research.

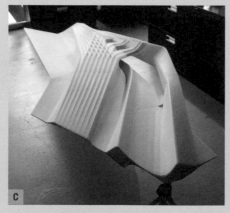

C

D

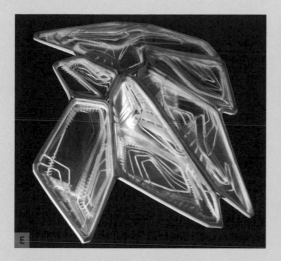

The hybridization of analogue and digital techniques has afforded designers the opportunity to radically transform the nature of their practice and output. EMERGENT/Tom Wiscombe's recent research into the spatial and ornamental potentials of airflow, fluid flow and glow illustrates the 'extreme integration' he has proposed for internal infrastructural systems in architecture. The three prototypes below each explore different aspects of this approach.

E AND F Tracery Glass reconsiders stained glass in contemporary architecture. Rather than dematerializing, this is not only not glass (it's polycarbonate), it is characterized by embedded technology which does both ornamental and physical work. It allows views, but does so through layers of light, relief, coils, PV panels and gradient colour patterns.

G AND H Thermo-strut intertwines welded-up plate-steel beams with fibre-composite shells embedded in solar-thermal tracery. The solar thermal system is a continuous loop that weaves around through the steel sections, forcing structural adaptations at intersections. The result is a prototype that organizes structural forces, fluid flows, and material properties into a tectonically coherent, yet ornamental assembly. This prototype is intended to take 'surface-to-strand' geometries to the next level, where disciplinary forces temper abstract formal sensibilities.

I AND J Lizard Panel, based partially on the skin of the Australian Agamid Lizard, is a puzzle-piece system with socketed structural and mechanical members for continuity. It is characterized by a lacy, meandering pattern of algae pipes for energy generation, as well as deep channels which collect greywater from rainfall. Algae and greywater systems interweave in a way that produces emergent structural behaviour.

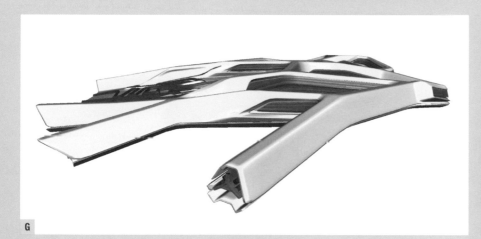

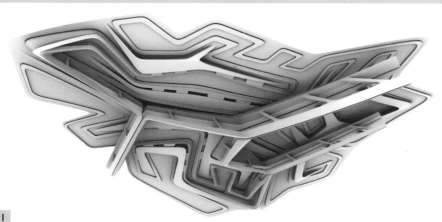

Case study Integrating digital and analogue fabrication techniques

Future Cities Lab – *Glaciarium*, New York, 2009.

Conceived as a portable interactive instrument to engage visitors' senses through the sight and sound of a melting ice core, the *Glaciarium* is a digitally designed and fabricated installation using techniques with a wider applicability for architecture. The project comprises two unique, asymmetrical layers, each with specific functions and formal intentions. The inner layer consists of spirals of triangulated laser-cut skins, and was assembled from hundreds of bespoke pieces folded and fused along their edges to create a seamless, translucent surface. Because this layer would be seen from the interior of the eyepiece, it had to be as light and ephemeral as possible. This inner layer was then suspended from an outer layer, constructed of soldered stainless steel. This lattice was initially formed in three pieces over the top of a complex CNC-milled particleboard jig that guided the geometry and aided the soldering process. The jig provided a precise and durable way to create complex and irregular lattices. The three lattices were then placed around the inner layer and were fused together in situ. The remainder of the components – including speakers, electronics, LEDs and sensors – were supported using laser-cut acrylic components.

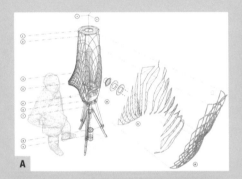
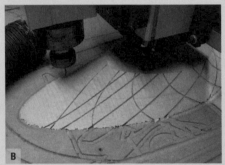

A Schematic 'exploded' drawing, showing components of the installation piece.

B CNC milling to produce the jig elements.

C Jig elements are combined together to provide formwork, upon which the frame may be assembled.

D Stainless-steel rods are run along the grooves of the formwork and soldered together, producing the frame.

E Laser-cut translucent plastic-sheet components are made following the digital cutting pattern.

F These are then connected to produce a seamless skin, or lantern, to sit within the stainless-steel frame. listening to the effects of the melting ice core.

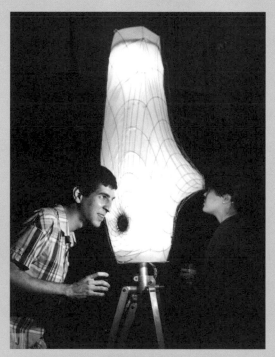

G The ice core is installed within the lantern.

H Close-up view of the exterior of frame and lantern.

I Internal view, illustrating the spiralling patterns of the laser-cut pieces forming the lantern skin.

J Final installation, with viewers observing and listening to the effects of the melting ice core.

Case study Translating between sound and architecture

Misha Smith – Prototype for a Spatialized Instrument, 2010.

For his diploma design thesis, Misha Smith developed a project on 'performing buildings'. The theme of his chosen studio programme at the Bartlett was '(extra) ordinary', and led to inquiries on the seamless hybrid of digital and real space. He proposes a flexible, sonic architecture that may be installed in different locations and configurations to provide an experiential transformation of space. The final design is a hybrid of analogue and digital methods, using digital fabrication techniques to produce analogue mechanical notes – further evolved through interactive digital technology. The digital processes applied enable the design and manufacture of complex forms that would be manually time-consuming. Given the performative nature of the installation, the project also taught the designer about the constraints, potential and difficulties of processes, materials and techniques.

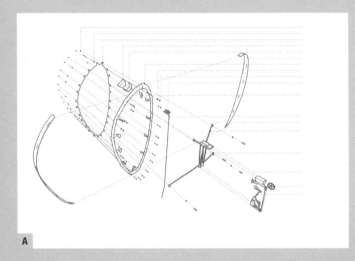

A

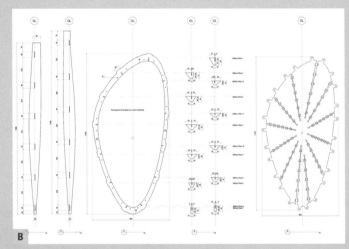

B

A Exploded axonometric CAD drawing showing the various components for the composite design.

B Detailed dimensions and cutting-pattern data for frame ring and soundboard.

C The soundboards are CNC-cut from birch plywood to produce flat components.

D The flat soundboards achieve curvature through the connection of the panels using an integrated pattern of holes.

E Mild-steel frame rings are laser-cut ready to form the frames.

F The frames are welded together using laser-cut frame edges, rings and stiffeners to produce the structure for the instrument.

C

D

E

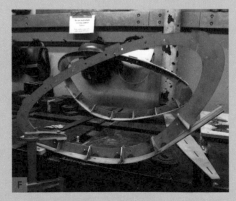

F

G, H AND I Tuning takes place as the analogue sound-producing mechanism and digitally fabricated shell and frame are connected together.

J Once tuned, the instruments may be installed in a variety of configurations and spaces, and further adjusted to optimize their impact on the experience of them.

3. Non-standard design and mass customization

Before the implementation of digital technologies, in particular CAD/CAM systems, the construction and assembly processes used in architecture were a direct consequence of industrial manufacturing and the logic of mass production and standardization. To be economically viable, building components made throughout the twentieth century were for the most part geometrically simple and limited in terms of type, since both geometrical complexity and variety typically resulted in exponential cost implications. This situation has been transformed through digital fabrication methods, wherein the multiplicity and complexity of design elements has no correlation to economies or efficiencies of production. Rather than mass production, this change towards the making of unique, highly variable components has led to the concept of 'mass customization', through which 'it is just as easy and cost-effective for a CNC milling machine to produce 1,000 unique objects as to produce 1,000 identical ones.'[1] With this in mind, it is easy to understand that the vast growth in differentiated parts for architectural design, uncoupled from the historical association of cost increase, has afforded designers unprecedented opportunities. Intrinsic to the notion of mass customization is the idea of 'non-standard' components. In opposition to the standardization of building elements, digital fabrication methods allow and positively encourage the making of one-off, non-standard objects and components. In an architectural context, using non-standard elements – whether structural, façade, internal or otherwise – means that the possibilities of optimizing variance in relation to ecological and local criteria, alongside other design intentions and aesthetic decisions, are myriad. To further our knowledge and understanding of this potential, let us now consider a number of different digital fabrication approaches and their applications.

1. Kolarevic, B. [ed.] (2003) *Architecture in the Digital Age: Design and Manufacturing*. Spon Press, p.52.

Non-standard design provided the primary area of research for Tim Marjot's design thesis on mass customized housing that could be delivered using a 'just-in-time' system of manufacture. The scale model shows non-standard façade panels – each altered in response to aesthetic choices, daylighting conditions and thermal capacity as required – that form an integrated surface. The detail view of the bricks highlights the complexity of the modular panels' geometry as they articulate an array of components.

Case study Pushing the limits of computational detail and ornament

Michael Hansmeyer – The Subdivided Column, 2010–11.

This project involves the design of a new column order based on subdivision processes. It explores how subdivision can define and embellish the column with an elaborate system of ornamentation. An abstracted Doric column is used as an input form to the subdivision processes. This geometric description conveys topological information about the form to be generated. The input form is tagged, allowing the subdivision process to distinguish between individual components. This enables a heterogeneous application of the process, with distinct local parameter settings. The result is a series of columns that exhibit both highly specific local conditions and an overall coherence and continuity. The ornament is in continuous flow, yet consists of distinct local formations. The complexity of 'column' contrasts with the simplicity of its generative process.

The processes can be understood by considering their two parts: topological rules and weighting rules. The topological rules specify how to obtain the combinatorics of the refined mesh from the combinatorics of the input mesh by generating new vertices, edges and faces. The weighting rules specify how to calculate the positions of these new vertices based on interpolation between vertices of the input mesh. By introducing parameters to allow for variations in these weighting rules, non-rounded forms with highly diverse attributes can be produced. Whereas the traditional weighting rules specify the positions of new vertices strictly as interpolations of previous-generation vertices, these rules are amended to allow for extrusion along face, edge and vertex normals. It is primarily through these changes to the established schemes that the complex geometries in this project become possible.

A

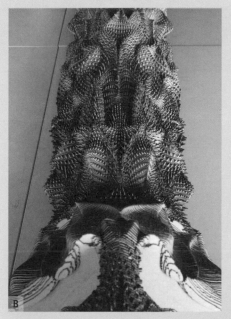

B

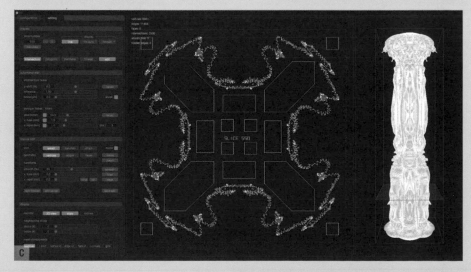

C

A The subdivided columns exhibit an extraordinarily complex geometry. Each comprises between 4 million and 32 million faces. Not only do the valences of the vertices vary throughout their mesh, but surfaces frequently intersect each other. In addition, the surfaces are not necessarily continuous. Several fabrication options for a full-size, 3m-high column were considered. A first option, 3D printing, was deemed too expensive at this scale (most 3D printing applications are anyway unable to handle such large polygon counts). A second option was 6-axis CNC milling. This, however, would not have been able to reproduce the tight radii of the column's concave and convex surfaces. The final consideration was a layered model. While labour-intensive to produce, it enables very accurate reproduction of the generated geometries.

B The column shown uses 2,700 slices of 1mm paperboard. Slices are hollowed out to reduce weight, and they have four consistent holes so that they can be positioned on steel rods. This not only facilitates their assembly and alignment, but provides the column with extra stability and precludes the need to glue slices together. The negative of the slices is saved to allow for future mould creation.

C A program was written specifically to compute the outlines of the subdivided columns at each layer. It intersected the surfaces of the form with a plane, to form a slice. The resulting intersection lines were combined into polygons, which in turn were filtered according to minimum area and a polygon-in polygon test. Further tests scanned for self-intersecting among the polygons, in which case an offset filter was applied. In addition, the minimum surface width of convex branches was regulated to ensure that pieces of the slice did not break off. The resulting outline was written to a file and sent to a laser printer.

Case study Non-standard fabrication and interactive surfaces

dECOi/Mark Goulthorpe – HypoSurface, various locations, 1999–present.

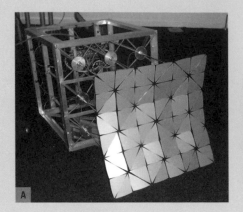

A First 9-actuator Hypo 1 prototype with spring-loaded pneumatic actuators and aluminum/rubber faceted skin.

B First multi-module testing of 560-actuator Hypo 2 prototype.

C, D AND E Sequential development of modular Hypo2 rubber and aluminum skin elements, from digital design to 1:1 physical prototypes.

The generation and development of a dynamic architectural surface is the driving force behind this ongoing project. Using a matrix of computer-controlled actuators, a large surface can be deformed at high speed, providing an immediately responsive formal plasticity. The architecture thus explored is reciprocally adaptive to people, or 'alloplastic'. It develops an understanding of the effect of animate form, and enables a range of interactive systems to elicit various modes of engagement. These interactive interfaces are sophisticated parametric systems, presenting extraordinary nuance and differentiation to the generation of movement and sound: an extreme case study of multimedia digital architecture. The essential feature of HypoSurface is that it moves, opening up a new medium of animate form for the plastic arts and architecture. Through collaboration with specialist roboticists, mathematicians and programmers, dECOi developed the base system of pneumatic actuators via a series of evolving prototypes. The geometry and elasticity of the flexible surface, capable of deformation of 600mm with waves of 100km per hour, required focused consideration to evolve a highly performative modular rubber-and-metal 'voxel'. Perhaps of greater significance than the mechanical development has been the augmentation of the computational control systems to afford the level of interactivity required.

F TO Q Movement interactivity at BIO biotechnology
conference, Boston, USA, 2006.

Below and bottom
Digital fabrication has led to
a revival of craft albeit with
a new and interdisciplinary
understanding pertaining to the
algorithmic and precise qualities
that digital technologies may
couple with more conventional
methods of creative practice.
As such, the artist Kumiko
Shimizu's Angry House project
posits the notion of the human
and the digital in a fluctuating
relationship that concerns a rich
dialogue between both analogue
and digital design and fabrication
techniques. Envisaged as a full-
size pavilion, it is shown here
as a laser-cut acrylic model and
CNC-milled timber prototype.

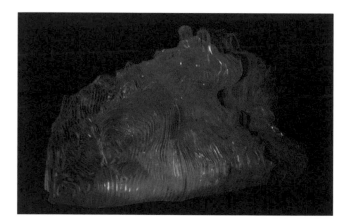

4. Digital fabrication principles

The techniques of digital fabrication generally fit into four main categories: cutting, subtraction, addition and formation. These headings are analogous to traditional processes used in architectural modelmaking and even full-sized prototyping, wherein materials are manually worked with tools to achieve the desired results.[2] However, it is useful at this point to understand the differences between these procedures before we start to discuss the various equipment and machines that facilitate them.

2. For a comprehensive discussion of the different media, types and applications for physical modelmaking in architecture, see Dunn, N. (2010) *Architectural Modelmaking*. Laurence King.

Cutting

Perhaps the most accessible and commonly applied method of digital fabrication is 'cutting'. There is a range of different cutting techniques, but essentially they all enable the production of flat components using a cutting head that follows instructions provided by digital design data to make shaped elements from sheet materials. The cutting head and sheet material move along two axes in relation to each other. This may be as a result of a moving cutting head, a moving bed upon which the material lies or, occasionally, a combination of both. Sometimes referred to as 'two-dimensional fabrication', CAD/CAM cutting techniques are usually limited by the thickness of material they can cut, which generates different cutting technologies for different materials. Laser-beam, plasma-arc and water-jet are all types of cutting technology that permit specific applications. The use of laser beams to cut materials is a widely known and available method, and will be dealt with in considerable detail later in this section. At this stage, it is only necessary to know that the process focuses a high-intensity beam of infrared light mixed with a stream of highly pressurized gas, usually carbon dioxide, to cut materials. The plasma-arc cutting process passes an electric arc through a compressed gas jet in the machine's cutting head, which heats the gas into very high-temperature plasma, a state change that subsequently reverses as the heat is transferred to cut the material. Water jets, as the name implies, force a high-pressured jet of water, mixed with an abrasive, through the cutting head, slicing the material in a precise manner.

Subtraction

Fabrication methods using a subtractive process take material from an existing solid volume, leaving behind the desired features and components. The excess material is typically removed through a milling or routing process. These machines are available with a range of axially constrained cutting heads depending on the required task. Two-axis milling machines work by having the rotating drill bit move along X and Y axes, thereby subtracting two-dimensional patterns of material. The addition of another axis, as featured in three-axis machines, enables the drill bit to be moved up and down along the Z axis, allowing material to be subtracted volumetrically. This process is a logical extension of the two-axis method, and whilst it has greater application in CAD/CAM techniques it is still fairly limited in terms of the components it can make. It is therefore with four- and five-axis machines that complex forms and surface features may be produced, as these augment the milling or routing process through further manipulation of either the cutting head or the cutting bed by providing additional axes of rotation. Furthermore, the drill bits within the cutting heads come in different sizes, similar to conventional drills, allowing for a variety of finishes and accuracy. Likewise, the milling or routing may be applied at various speeds in relation to the material's characteristics.

Subtractive processes using conventional machines have advantages in relation to:
*   Component size – as much larger elements can be made with these machines.
*   Material selection – as a wider range of raw material can be used.
*   Precision – as more accurate elements can be fabricated due to lower tolerances.
*   Production – as these machines are typically more economical and faster for larger quantities of elements.

Addition

In direct contrast to the above methods, fabrication processes based on an additive technique slowly build up material in layers rather than steadily removing it. This category of digital fabrication is most commonly known as rapid prototyping, though this is actually an umbrella term that includes a number of different techniques. However, all additive processes work on the basis of translating digital design information into a series of two-dimensional layers. The data of each individual layer is then used to direct the head of the fabrication machine, and the physical object is made through an accumulative process of layering.

Additive processes have advantages in relation to:
*   Bespoke components – the direct conversion from digital model (usually to an .stl file format) means that no additional devices such as jibs or moulds are required for the efficient fabrication of unique elements.
*   Complex form – since material is deposited at all required points to produce the element, allowing sophisticated geometry and internal voids to be easily fabricated.
*   Fabrication environment – rapid prototyping machines are typically enclosed and quiet in operation enabling them to be installed in design studios.
*   Non-expert use – since techniques such as rapid prototyping do not require users to have obtained specialist programming languages or machine skills prior to application.

Formation

Rather than removing or building up material, formative fabrication processes utilize mechanical forces to reshape or deform materials into the required shape. Heat or steam is typically used in such processes, to render the material being formed more pliable and then to retain its new geometry once it has cooled.

5. Laser cutting

Perhaps the most familiar and accessible form of digital fabrication is laser cutting. An increasingly common machine within the workshops of architecture schools, professional model makers and even design practices, the laser cutter is an important tool owing to the array of functions it offers. Laser cutters are suitable for use with comparatively thin materials, usually up to 20mm thick, but provide a high degree of accuracy and clean, square-edged cuts. In addition, laser cutting may be used with a range of materials, including paper, card, plastics, wood, metals (such as aluminium, brass, mild and stainless steel) and even textiles. The precision offered by this method enables the designer to make components with complex shapes and detailed elements, incorporating apertures and patterns, even at relatively small scales. This last-named advantage initially attracted a number of professional model makers to its use in the making of high-quality model components such as those for façades, although it has since become much more prevalent. Unless applied at an industrial scale, most laser cutters are relatively small, which places clear limits on the size of components that may be fabricated.

The fabrication process of laser cutting is perhaps most analogous with conventional methods of physical modelmaking and prototyping, since components are cut from a sheet material and then assembled to form three-dimensional propositions. The only real differences lie in the choice of materials and precision with which

Below
This model by Bjarke Ingels Group (BIG) for their design of the REN building, Shanghai, utilized laser-cut plastic sheet to enable the intricate façade pattern and curvilinear geometry to be produced with precision.

Bottom right
Laser cutters are available in a range of shapes and sizes, but all work on the same principle in that there is a protective casing (top) which houses the laser moving across a metal grill (bottom), upon which the material to be cut is placed.

curvilinear and detailed parts are cut, which would be much more difficult to achieve using traditional tools such as craft knives or scalpels. As such, the way of thinking on behalf of designers is similar to that adopted when making models and installations manually, as they need to visualize the three-dimensional form prior to setting out the different components on the sheet ready to be cut – a process also analogous to pattern cutting in fashion design. Of course the computer is instrumental in this regard, enabling designers to translate information from the three-dimensional digital to the two-dimensional sheets, which once cut provide a kit of parts to be assembled as required. This process of construction is akin to traditional methods, except that some designers use the laser-cutting technology to provide a reference key on each component as well as small holes, slots and notches to aid assembly. This brings us to another key feature of this digital fabrication technique: the ability to score or etch onto the surface of materials. Because the power of the laser is highly controllable and may be applied in a very accurate manner, it does not necessarily cut the material but may be used to inscribe patterns, texture or the location of primary elements (for example, window positions on a façade) in order to further enhance the aesthetic information of the components. Such application can be a time-consuming process, so it is important to specify data that is integral to the components and avoid unnecessary ornamentation where possible.

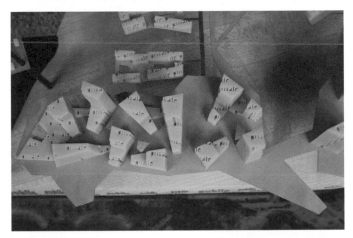

Top and middle two
The use of laser-cutting technology was combined with laser sintering and CNC milling to produce the 'floating' planes of landscape and programme in this masterplan model for Almere Dune designed by ZUS (Zones Urbaines Sensibles). A visually striking object in its own right, the model employs digitally driven fabrication techniques to give legibility and detail to small components within the overall composition.

Bottom
Modelmaking at Coop Himmelb(l)au for their Musée des Confluences, Lyons, utilizes laser-cut and scored panels to achieve the surface geometry of the building's design.

Right
Barkow Leibinger designed these complex three-dimensional objects, drawn in 3D modelling software, as part of an investigation into the materiality of interior components that could be decorative, enable lighting effects and retain structural integrity.

Middle
The objects were fabricated using a revolving laser-cutting technique which rotates the material as well as cutting it, allowing complex shapes to be cut from three-dimensional objects rather than two-dimensional sheets of material.

Below and bottom right
In this project for street furniture in Manchester, the designer Rupert Griffiths used digital design and laser cutting to produce the objects. From left to right:
1 CAD drawing of foliage wrapping around base of tree.
2 Full-size prototype in the artist's studio for evaluation.
3 Final object installed in public realm.

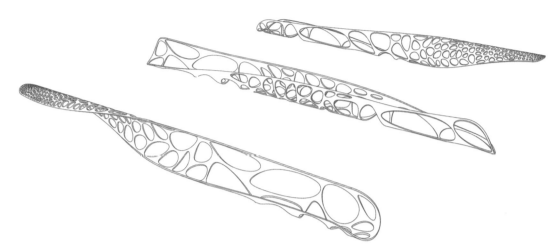

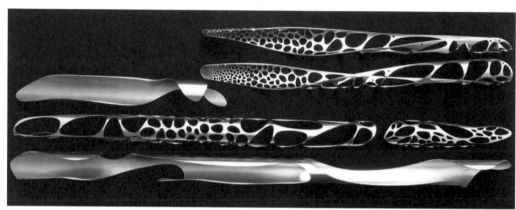

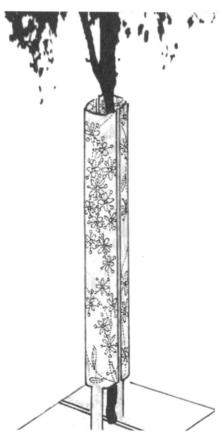

Case study Plasma-cut shelter

sixteen*(makers) – 55/02, Kielder Water and Forest Park, Northumberland, 2009.

Accompanying their research and design project at Kielder (see page 125 for details), sixteen*(makers) designed 55/02 in collaboration with steel manufacturers Stahlbogen GmbH. The small structure (named after its position coordinates) offers both shelter and an engagement with the landscape, addressing visitors to the specific qualities of its location.

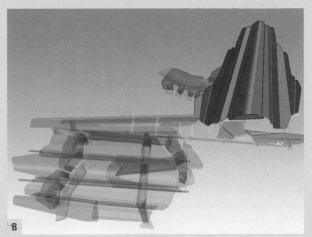

A Physical scale model at 1:100, showing arrangement of folded planes.

B The design is developed in detail using 3D CAD modelling to enable the folded panels and structure to be integrated accurately.

C The CNC plasma-cut panels are folded as specified at the manufacturers, and connected.

D Because of these folds, the panels have structural rigidity and integrity and can be freestanding elements.

E The panels are powder coated to protect from weathering and lifted into position on site, where they are connected to pad foundations and, in the case of overhead panels, supporting steel structures.

F The final shelter in context.

Case study Laser-cutting process as generative mode of design
Barkow Leibinger – Gatehouse, Stuttgart, 2007

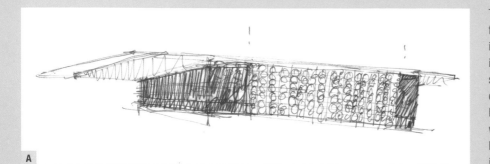

A

The Gatehouse uses laser digital cutting to fabricate a unique and freestanding building, in which the application of this technique is integral to the construction and not simply surface decoration. Citing as precedent the work of Jean Prouvé – such as his 1950s factory in Maxville, wherein entire building components were constructed using sheet metal – Barkow Leibinger and their client Trumpf, who specialize in laser-cutting technologies, developed a series of workshops to explore the fabrication possibilities of laser-cut and welded sheet metal. The 32 x 11m stainless-steel roof cantilevers 22m from four columns, resulting in a 600mm-deep honeycombed box-beam of 3mm stainless and mild steel. The triangular roof-plane perforations vary in density in correlation to weight reduction along the cantilever's length. The roof is thus a mathematical diagram explicitly illustrating the loading across the structure.

A Concept sketch.

B, C, D AND E Various roof patterns were explored through laser-cut scale models, to refine surface geometry and relationship of apertures across the roof plane.

F 1:50 mild-steel prototype, fabricated to explore structural implications in relation to triangulation.

G Full-scale fabrication of roof structure indicates its size.

B

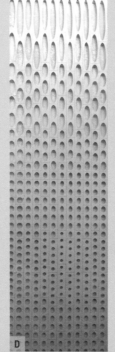

C

D

E

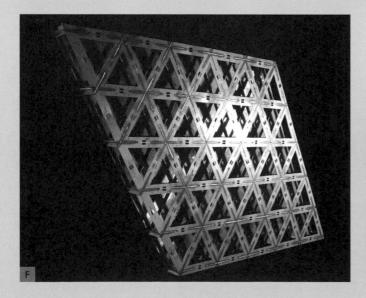

F

G

H The roof comprises 204 cassettes, 700 x 3,000mm, fastened together forming a continuous stiff plane. These components arrive on site as a series of prefabricated 32m strips bolted together, are raised as a unified roof up and over the columns and then fastened to pin-joints.

I Prototype detail section of roof structure for testing prior to full fabrication.

J Close-up view of roof structure prior to application of stainless-steel cladding.

K The underside of the roof is accentuated by illuminating the coffers with LED lighting, further enhancing the structure's 'floating' appearance. Backlighting the façades ensures that the gatehouse functions as an entrance 'lantern' at night.

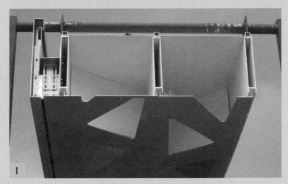

6. CNC milling and routing

Computer Numerically Controlled (CNC) milling and routing are two of the most firmly established digital fabrication techniques, with a 40-year history in relation to architecture. Although specifically used as a 'prefix' for these applications, the CNC process actually underlies most digital making technologies since it uses a computer system to generate coded instructions that in turn control the movements of a machine tool. This basic explanation shadows a complex procedure in which the CNC program coordinates a number of different tasks at any given time, including motion control, tool changes and spindle operation. Here we begin to encounter the vast array of options available to designers when organizing the movement and operation of the milling or routing head. This sequence of control functions is known as the 'tool path', and provides a set of instructions for the machine. The milling or routing of materials may be achieved in an almost endless number of ways, and even small variations in the instructions may produce significant differences in the end products. This is one of the main reasons that a skilled workshop technician or machine operator may prove valuable to the process, particularly where machinery has four or five axes in use and the operational parameters may become highly involved. CNC commands are effectively short computer scripts that tell the machine what to do. The majority of these functions are typically designated with a letter 'G', and as a consequence CAD/CAM technicians often refer to CNC instructions as 'G-code'. These instructions, also known as preparatory codes, are typically divided into several primary commands such as a rapid move, a controlled move in a straight line or arc, a series of controlled moves (resulting in a cut, hole or profile), or to set tool information. The command combinations directly affect the fabrication process and thus any manufactured components.

CNC milling or routing has two main roles. In its first, and perhaps most immediate, use it may be applied to remove material from a volume and fabricate components in a manner similar to carving, i.e. the material forms that remain on the machine bed are the desired design components. Architectural designers, keen to achieve complex geometries and fluid aesthetics with precision and efficiency, have readily exploited this process. Since the G-code interface may be used to maximize the arrangement and number of different components produced from a volume of material, this process may also reduce the amount of waste material and facilitates effective and relatively economical making of non-standard components. Such optimization is core to the growth of this digital fabrication technology within design disciplines, because it allows the material volume to be fully used within its limits. The second application

for CNC milling or routing relates to the results of the process rather than being an end in itself. The high degree of accuracy and complexity of surfaces and forms that may be fabricated using this method means that it is also able to make geometrically sophisticated and very detailed moulds. These moulds may then be used to cast other materials, and are therefore often a key element in formative fabrication methods. Milling and routing processes are similar since they both use a rotating cutter to subtract material, but whereas milling is useful for metals amongst other materials, routing is typically applied only to wood and plastics. Because of the comparative density of these materials, the router cutting head is able to remove a much larger amount of them in a given time frame. As a direct consequence, specific machine types have been developed that increasingly differ from those used for working metals.

Routing is actually a parent term that includes numerous machine operations such as drilling, grooving and shaping of materials. The machine designs vary from relatively small tabletop versions appropriate for modelmaking to large machines able to handle and finish components typically up to 1.5m in each direction. Industrial manufacturing equipment may go well beyond these limits dependent on the production process and elements required. The most commonly used machines are three- and five-axis types. Although three-axis control should enable the cutting head to access any desired point within the work field, these operations are often limited due to obstruction by the actual component being fabricated. Five-axis machines therefore provide a further two rotational axes, perpendicular to one another, which facilitates the cutting head to reach internal areas or overhangs etc. Many applications of the routing process involve sheet materials, such as plywood or MDF, and therefore the work field is usually greater in the X and Y axes than the Z axis. Gantry configurations of machines are the most widespread, featuring either a fixed or moving worktable upon which the material is mounted. The advantages of moving worktables over their fixed counterparts are that they are often more economical and even precise but they are constrained by the size and weight of the element being fabricated. Fixed worktable set-ups overcome these limits through the use of a moving gantry but such operation needs to be able to move with precision and speed whilst withstanding the forces encountered during cutting.

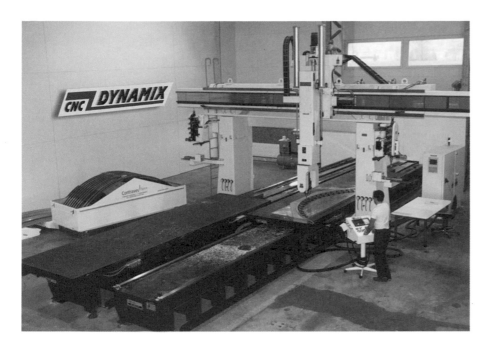

Above
CNC milling and routing machines come in a range of sizes and types, depending on the purpose and materials intended for processing.

Below
The most common type of CNC milling and routing machines are the gantry type, shown here, which may be used to cut a variety of materials through a simple change of tool bits in the machine head.

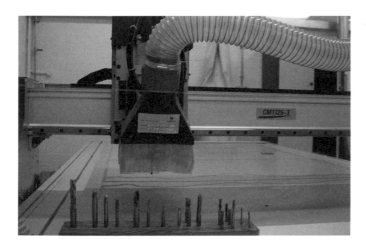

TIP LAYOUT SHEETS

A simple error when transferring digital design data for use with sheet-material fabrication processes is the layout sheets not being 'flat' in CAD space. This can easily be rectified by aligning the Z axis to zero prior to machining.

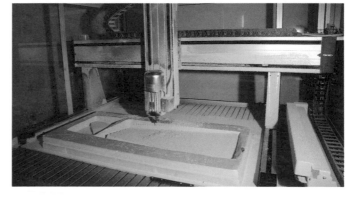

STEP BY STEP CNC MILLING

This domestic garden shelter, designed by John Bridge, illustrates the design and fabrication process undertaken, with emphasis on CNC milling as an integral part of the manufacturing path.

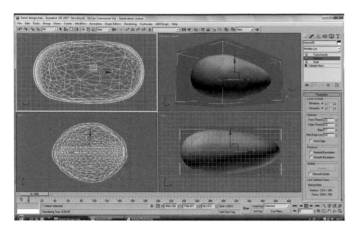

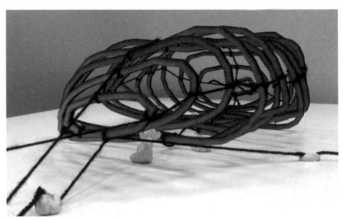

1 The design was initially developed digitally in relation to the maximum size of plywood sheets able to fit on the CNC milling bed. Starting with a cuboid form, a sphere was 'grown' from the epicentre, and by applying modifiers the spherical form was pulled towards the internal, cuboid geometry.

2 Prior to full-size fabrication, the design was tested using a laser-cut MDF scale model that simulated the proposed method of manufacture and enabled potential issues to be identified. It transpired that structural stability was a major problem since the ribs were in one plane only. This led to the development of cross-sectional ribs, affording easy assembly and rigidity.

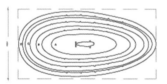

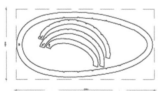

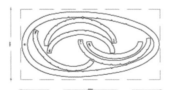

4 Any drawing errors in the sheet files are typically identified in the CNC machine's software, but care should be taken to ensure that the data is correctly formatted. Using the cutting patterns, or toolpaths, from the CAD/CAM files, the CNC milling machine cuts the full-size components from 18mm plywood sheets.

3 Once all the components were drawn in CAD software, sheets were prepared for 'file-to-factory' order. A specific package optimized the number of components from each sheet, reducing material waste.

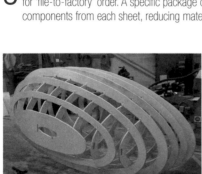

5 The components are slotted and jointed together. Assembly may be greatly assisted by using the CNC machine to provide reference numbers and pre-cut holes and slots.

6 To protect the wood from weathering, a UVi polythene skin was stapled and glued to the structural shell to allow outdoor usage.

Operations

The form and size of the cutting tool itself distinguishes the various machining operations possible with routers. As with the majority of CNC machines, tool changing is often an automatic procedure carried out under part-program control. First-generation three-axis machines provided general routing processes including drilling and edge profiling, but current five-axis configurations have extended this range to include sawing, contouring and carving.

The wide range of machining operations achievable with routers is informed by size and form of the cutting tool. Part-program control within the G-code instructions typically includes tool changing automatically as is the case with most CNC machines. While three-axis machines are effective for general routing procedures such as drilling and edge profiling, five-axis versions extend these operations further to facilitate carving, contouring and sawing. The primary process of routing uses a fluted cutter, typically less than 25mm in diameter, which rotates at high speed to remove material. An almost limitless combination and types of shapes and apertures may be achieved due to the spectrum of different cutter geometries available but it is worth understanding the main applications:

- Drilling or boring – this is perhaps the most familiar process. Small diameter holes are made using a corresponding sized router, which is sunk into the material as with a conventional drill. A large diameter hole may be produced by routing along its perimeter outline and then removing the waste disc left behind.

- Carving – this is implemented to fabricate contoured 3D surfaces that may feature complex curvilinear geometry. This process may involve several different types of cutter in any single application. Excess material is first removed using a ball-nose cutter and then once the rough shape has been carved, pointed detail tools are used to create intricate surface features and a high level of finish.

- Shaping – this is applied to fabricate profiles on edges, both internal and external, typically with a better level of finish and efficiency than routing. Cutter diameters may be up to 150mm and above, which coupled with interchangeable blades enable complex profiles to be produced.

- Sanding – this may be used to finish profiled edges etc. and is achieved through a sanding head which is similar to a shaping head, providing components ready for assembly.

- Sawing – where large quantities of linear cuts are required, routers may lose their efficiency in relation to other equipment such as circular saws but a number of tooling attachments are now available to augment routing operations if required.

- Squaring – this is possible by oscillating scraper blades across the work field and is used to remove significant excess material that would be inefficient or inaccessible to remove using other routing or cutting procedures.

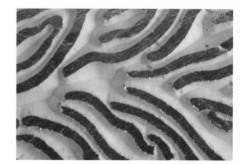

CNC milling enables designers to fabricate components with highly intricate surface features, as shown in this work by Rupert Griffiths.

STEP BY STEP MAKING A PAVILION

Prototype Unit, Manchester School of Architecture – Reflective Room, Manchester Museum, 2010.

This temporary structure provides a public 'room', formed by two interlocking wall elements, that includes a continuous bench, allowing users pause and a respite from the city. Designed and constructed by students from the Prototype Unit led by Ming Chung and Nick Tyson, the design and fabrication process utilized a range of media and techniques.

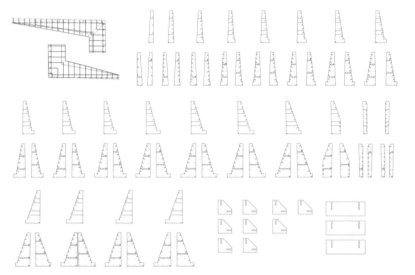

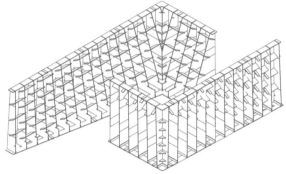

1 Initial design ideas used CAD software, producing laser-cut 1:10-scale models that enabled testing of three-dimensional structure and assembly methods.

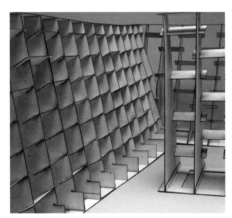

2 Following this stage, full-size prototypes were fabricated using manual and digital tools to allow detail connections to be resolved and material properties to be assessed. Structural considerations were reviewed and tested at 1:1 alongside preliminary calculations by Atelier One Engineers. This facilitated the optimizing of both material effects and structural assembly.

3 Standard-grade external plywood was selected as an appropriate material for the structural carcass, and finer-grade birch ply for the skin. This design cycle of prototype making, testing and adjustment directly informed the development of two-dimensional CAD design drawings.

The two-dimensional design drawings, converted to a three-dimensional CAD model, were used to test the assembly of components and enable structural calculations to be finalized. A tectonic system was established that utilized components cut from a flat sheet material and a dry slot-jointed construction method that provided an overall structural matrix. Vertical 'rib' and horizontal 'tab' standard-grade plywood components formed an external carcass that supported a synclastic curved plywood interior skin, embedded with standard glazed ceramic tiles. The plywood components were precision machined using a CNC router, and assembled by hand. The router was selected as an appropriate machine tool owing to the precision required for the dry-slot assembly and its ability to meet production demands within the allocated timeframe. Individual components from the three-dimensional CAD model were converted to two-dimensional templates in ArtCAM to set tool paths and optimize layouts on plywood sheets.

4 A workshop-based prefabrication sequence for component parts was predetermined by the sequence of assembly on site, and established batching for manufacture and delivery.

5 Manual prefabrication methods of cross lamination for the larger 'rib' and 'skin' components were developed as a consequence of the standard sheet dimensions and the limitations of the CNC router. Site work commenced with the installation of 'base plates' that provided a precise setting-out template for manual assembly of the 'rib' and 'tab' components.

6 The 'skin' layers were manufactured oversized, allowing on-site adjustments to accommodate the geometries of the synclastic, curved surface. Manual construction skills allowed adjustment to take place in order to resolve problems found on site.

7. Rapid prototyping

The best-known additive process in digital fabrication is rapid prototyping, which facilitates the quick production of objects from a range of materials depending on factors of time, cost and application. 'Rapid prototyping' is often mistakenly used as shorthand for a specific type of additive fabrication, but is a generic term within which a family of different methods are related.

The commonality of the various processes lies in the gradual build-up of incremental two-dimensional layers of material to produce a three-dimensional object. The first commercially available rapid-prototyping technique was Stereolithography in the late 1980s. Stereolithography, often abbreviated to SLA, uses liquid polymers that change state and solidify when laser light is traced across them. Each layer is 'drawn' by the laser across a tank of light-sensitive liquid polymer, resulting in a solid cross-section of material in relation to the laser's motion and outline. Once a layer has been made, a small platform inside the machine lowers it beneath the surface of the liquid and this process is repeated until all the necessary layers have been drawn and stacked together, thereby producing the final form. This object is then treated to remove any excess liquid and provide a more robust product.

The process of 3D printing is perhaps the most commonly known type of rapid prototyping, as it is frequently referred to under its parent term. In this digital fabrication method, layers of starch or ceramic powder are bonded to make objects. Although the models and components thus manufactured may be cleaned and sealed with an agent to improve their durability, they remain comparatively fragile and their surfaces have a tendency to granulate when handled. More substantial physical results are possible using additive fabrication processes, but 3D printing currently appears the most popular. Laminated Object Manufacturing (LOM) employs sheet material, usually paper or plastic, which is laser cut and then laminated together to form physical artefacts. The process of Fused Deposition Modelling (FDM) fabricates objects by melting a plastic filament that subsequently solidifies as a result

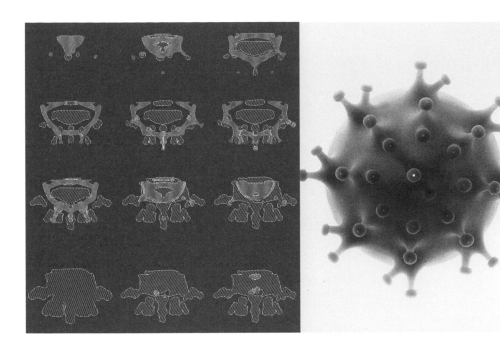

Left
The work of sixteen*(makers) has long engaged with digital technologies as an integral part of their design research and practice – as exemplified by this rapid-prototyped component for the project STAC. The sectional CAD drawings (left) illustrate the data used by stereolithography to build the complex three-dimensional object (right).

Below
Images of a rapid-prototyped model for Paul Broadbent's Bartlett diploma design thesis, Click-To-Play. The adaptive nature of the project, which related to notions of flux and reordering, produced a design that embraces fluid and ephemeral elements alongside more static ones.

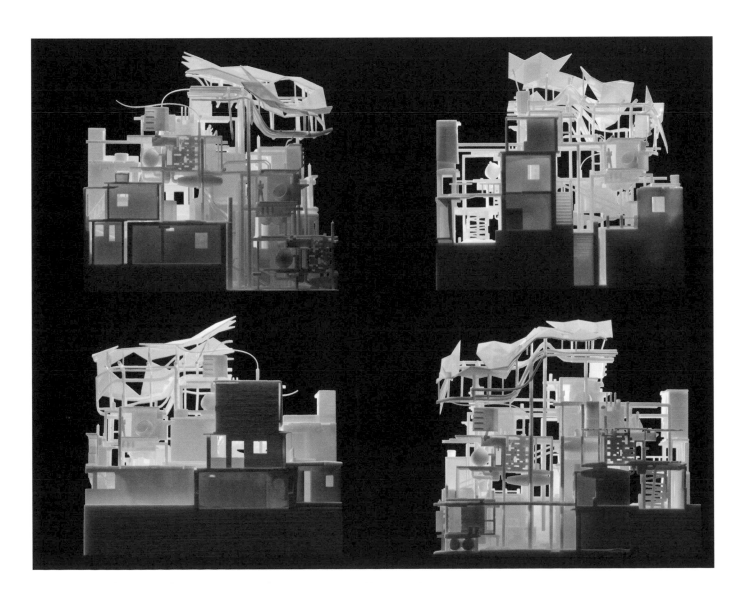

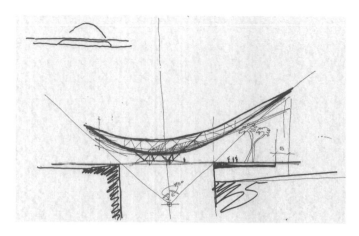

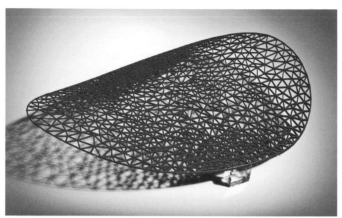

Above

Rogers Stirk Harbour + Partners use rapid-prototyping technology at various scales as a mode of design inquiry. This concept sketch and 3D print of the roof structure for the Santa Maria del Pianto metro station, Naples, represent stages in the design process that 'bookend' the evolutionary, algorithmic design as shown on page 60. The model enables the physicality and shading of the roof lattice to be further appreciated.

Below

Similarly, in order to communicate and test the design for the Leadenhall Building, rapid-prototyping techniques, in this case SLS (selective laser sintering) were employed to fabricate 1:50-scale 3D prints of various iterations of the node points in the complex geometry of the external structure. This allowed architectural assessment of these geometries, and eased communication in the design team.

of cooling, to make layer upon layer of material to form objects. In a similar manner, the Multi-Jet Manufacture (MJM) technique utilizes a modified printing head to 'draw' with thin layers of melted thermoplastic wax, again gradually forming the object in a cumulative process. Selective Laser Sintering (SLS) adopts a parallel approach to the previous two methods, but because of the choice of material – in this case, metal powder – it requires a laser to melt it and develop the thin layers from this.

To date, the most significant limitation of rapid-prototyping processes has been the size of objects they are able to fabricate. This factor, further nuanced by the considerable expense of additive fabrication machines along with the relatively long time required to make the objects, has led to a reasonably narrow use in architecture. Their greatest application is typically during the design process, in which they allow the designer to examine complex and curvilinear geometries in physical formations rather than digital ones. Rapid prototyping is also used to fabricate components, which provide prototypical uses for replication via further processes such as moulding and casting. More recently, the process of contour crafting has seen designers, architects and engineers experiment with an additive method similar to FDM but using a fast-setting, compound material similar to concrete to produce full-sized rather than scaled layers. This last-named development is still in its infancy, but may lead to revolutionary changes in the way we make buildings if we are able to 'print' them from digital information.

In many respects, physical prototypes exhibit a clarity and legibility that few forms of visual representation can attain. Realized by plastic techniques, the virtue of the prototype lies in its interactivity and the subsequent critical response this initiates.

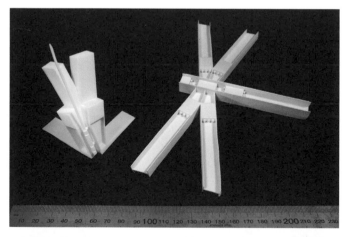

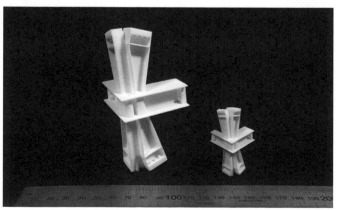

'Prototyping' design ideas. The complexity, relative ease and economic cost of rapid prototyping has allowed practitioners to use its techniques throughout the design process rather than simply to produce final models. This is much more synchronous with the process's application in other industries – typically, an iterative loop oscillating between design, prototype, revision and development toward a solution. For her Scared Womanhood diploma design thesis, Joanna Szulda used 3D printing to fabricate a final sectional model, shown here in relation to a digital render of the scheme. However, the digital production method was also used to generate explorative tools (middle right) as part of her design development and also to evaluate spaces and components in more detail, as illustrated in the 1:25-scale model (middle left).

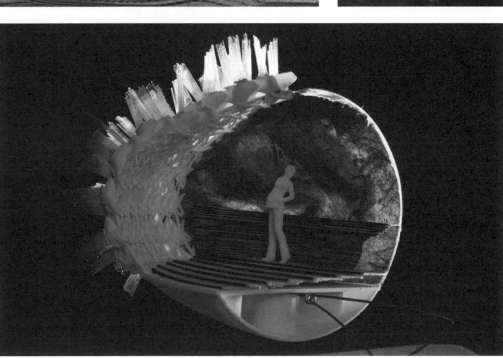

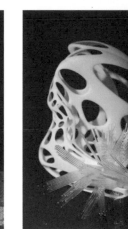

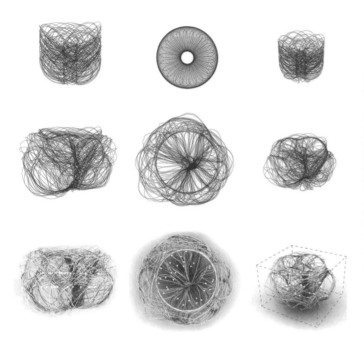

Above and bottom right

Rapid prototyping enables designers to produce complex geometries quickly and relatively economically. Through the interplay between scripting software and 3D printing, this speculative design by Archibureau/ Patrick Drewello evolves a creative dialogue between digital and analogue modes of production.

Right and bottom

Digital fabrication techniques have evolved significantly in their relatively short history; perhaps most exciting is the affordability of a number of these technologies and their potential implementation for architects and designers. The RepRap machine illustrated here was created by Dr Adrian Bowyer, a senior lecturer in mechanical engineering at the University of Bath, UK, in 2005. In stark contrast to even low-end commercial rapid-prototyping machines, RepRap has produced a 3D prototyping machine and accompanying free software that are economically viable for students and professionals alike. RepRap uses a variant of fused deposition modelling (FDM) technology, capable of printing plastic objects. Since many parts of the machine are made from plastic and it can print those parts, RepRap is a self-replicating machine – one that anyone can build given time and materials. For more information on how to build your own 3D printer see: http://reprap.org

Case study Printing full-size architectural design

Shiro Studio/D-Shape – Radiolaria Pavilion, Pontedera, Italy, 2008–11.

One of the most significant limitations for 3D printing lies in the maximum dimensions at which a machine can prototype objects. The ambition to 'print' a full-size building has driven the Italian engineer Enrico Dini to develop his d-shape technology and company. As with commercially available rapid-prototyping equipment, CAD drawings are translated by the d-shape into 3D layering. The machine deposits and binds layers 5–10mm deep, allowing building designs to be realized to minute tolerances.

A AND B The prototype machinery enables 1:1 sandstone buildings to be fabricated, using a stereolithography process that combines sand and an inorganic binder. The machine comprises a rigid 6m x 6m plan that lifts along four columns which may be extended, by adding parts, up to 12m in length.

C Andrea Morgante, founder of Shiro Studio, has collaborated with d-shape on the Radiolaria Pavilion, a complex, free-form structure produced using the world's largest 3D printer. The prototype shown here is scaled at 1:4 to evaluate the technology and design.

D The Radiolaria Pavilion aimed to define a complex, self-supporting structure that could demonstrate and test this pioneering construction technique. Measuring 3m x 3m x 3m, the structure represents a scale model of the final pavilion, to be 10m high and built in Pontedera, Italy.

A

B

C

D

8. 3D scanning

By contrast with the processes described above, three-dimensional (3D) scanning inverts the relationship between digital information and physical object. This technology reads information from existing physical sources, such as a model or building, and translates this into the computer as data, forming a digital version that may be furthered manipulated using appropriate software. In relation to the digital fabrication techniques discussed thus far this might seem counter-intuitive, but there may be significant advantages in this method. 3D scanning provides a 'bridge', across which design ideas may flow in an dialogue between physical modes of representation and digital design tools. A number of architectural designers retain a preference for physical models, and their designs may involve highly complex geometry and spatial arrangements. The importance of physical modelmaking cannot be overstated for architectural education and practice, and it has witnessed something of a renaissance in the last decade or so – frequently aided by digital fabrication techniques. Indeed, the tangible nature of physical models makes them highly versatile design tools, as they may be quickly produced and manipulated and allow a direct engagement with spatial features that are not always as easy to produce on a screen. In these situations, 3D scanners afford a translation of this design information rather than generation of it. Through the conversion of physical characteristics into digital data, this may be implemented in digital fabrication processes to make further models, prototypes and building components with a high degree of accuracy and formal integrity. This may seem an absorptive activity if we already have a physical object, but the important aspect here is the capacity of the computer to handle and refine digital geometry in a manner that would be extremely difficult to accomplish with the original artefact. By

Below
The use of a digitizer or digital arm may provide a key element of the design process, offering fluidity between different modes of inquiry and production. The physical model is first scanned by tracing the digital pen over its surface, so that the information of its physical features and geometry may be converted into digital data. Once this data is in the computer, software may be used to further transform it and manipulate the design in a manner that would be difficult to achieve using physical modelmaking techniques alone.

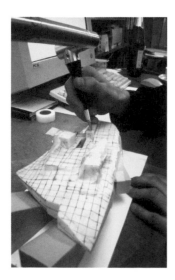
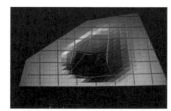

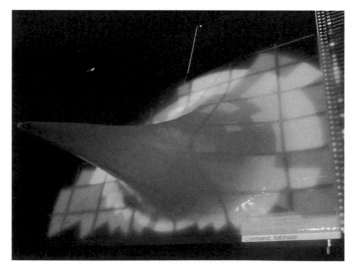

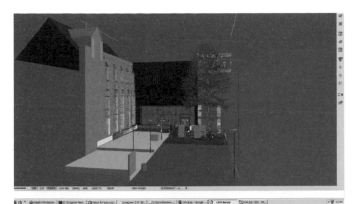

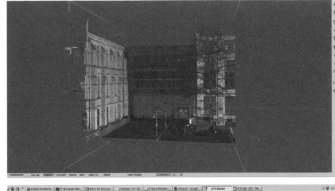

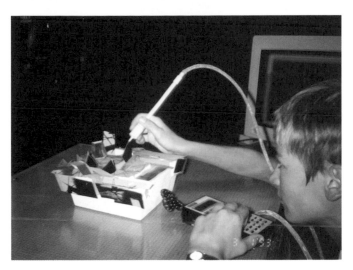

importing this information into the computer, a variety of software may be used to evaluate and optimize the design's properties in relation to, for example, material, structural, thermal and acoustic performance.

The technology of 3D scanners typically uses a laser to scan or 'read' the physical features of the object being translated. Depending on the type of object being scanned, the laser may be housed in a digitizer (sometimes referred to as a digitizing arm) or a tripod-mounted box similar to a camera. A digitizer enables the designer to guide the laser over the surface and spaces of small physical objects to gather data. In the case of less manually operated equipment, the scanner and tripod are set up and programmed to scan the required area, for example a building's façade, and do this in an autonomous fashion. Both these scanning approaches are known as 'reverse engineering'. The data from the physical artefact is assembled in the computer as a pattern of coordinates called a 'point cloud'. This arrangement of information is then translated using specialist software to provide a precise digital model of the original object. The digital model may then be exported to other CAD programs for further development or to integrate with other data as necessary.

Top left and right
3D laser scanning is transforming the way architects and the construction industry obtain site and contextual data. The accuracy of laser scanners to 'read' their environment and then, through conversion software, to make this data available for use in CAD programs allows designers to work with very precise information. It also enables speculative ideas to be tested three-dimensionally prior to implementation. This latter aspect has been particularly valuable in collision analyses, whereby engineers are able to check pipe routes, etc. in spaces that would traditionally be difficult to survey.

Above left and right
For their design of the East Pavilion at the Groninger Museum, Netherlands, Coop Himmelb(lau overlayed three-dimensional volumetric sketches which developed into a sketch model providing a first 'emotional imprint' of the concept. A digitizer was then used, enabling the designers to maintain the original gesture of the sketch model and fix it precisely within a three-dimensional grid. This process sought to capture the liveliness of the sketch and translate its sculptural details to the actual building. The digital model was subsequently enlarged step-by-step in order to consider structural and spatial details, and ultimately was used directly in the production of the pavilion parts.

Case study Digitizing architectural design
3XN – Louisiana Pavilion, 2009.

The Louisiana Pavilion was a collaborative project to build with biodegradable and energy-generating materials, creating an energy-self-sufficient architecture that also can be part of, and decompose within, the biological cycle after use. For the outer shell of the sculpture, glass-fibre composites were replaced with a bio composite from flax fibres cast in biological resin, whilst cork sheets replaced polystyrene foam for the inner core.

On top of the pavilion are placed 1mm-thick flexible solar cells cast in thin film, making them applicable to double-curved surfaces. Piezoelectric materials, which generate electric current from the weight of visitors, are laid in the floor. Combined, this gives the sculpture enough energy to power the integrated LED lights. The pavilion has a coating of hydrophilic nanoparticles that makes its surfaces self-cleaning: rainwater is dispersed beneath the dirt on the surface, leaving it cleaner.

A Design development through physical modelmaking, exploring curved forms and loops.

B Further development of the geometry, with loops becoming narrower in width.

C Digitizing the model to translate physical information into digital design data.

D Fabrication process: casting elements with 80mm cork core.

E Adapting the elements once removed from their moulds, including sanding and filling as necessary.

F First priming of a component.

G Pavilion form begins to emerge through text-assembly process.

H First layer of paint is applied prior to self-cleaning layer.

I The pavilion retains heat by using phase-changing materials. The material retains the sun's energy, releasing it when the temperature drops. When the temperature rises, the material absorbs energy and is liquefied at exactly 23 degrees Celsius. When temperature drops, it solidifies and releases energy. It is estimated that phase-changing materials can cut costs by 10–15 per cent on heating and cooling of buildings. Adapting new sustainable materials to digital modes of production was a huge challenge in itself. The learning process of substituting synthetic materials for biological counterparts spanned the entire project, revealing many obstacles and producing innovations on the way.

9. Robotics

Once the preserve of automotive and engineering industries, robotics is a burgeoning area of research and development in architectural production. The building industry has used robotics since the late 1970s but usually to facilitate construction operations rather than for fabrication. This situation has been transformed, predominantly through the pioneering work of a few architects and researchers who are investigating the application of 'articulated robots' for innovative design. These robots are capable of complex procedures and, in contrast to other digital fabrication methods, which are relatively fixed owing to the position of the machine bed or the equipment's own dimensional constraints, offer considerable flexibility. This flexibility is born of the robot's ability to work in a non-cubic space, self-referencing its position in relation to an object. In addition, the robot's 'hand', also referred to as the 'end effecter', may incorporate an array of tools and be programmed to accomplish very specific, sophisticated actions. Since robots may be manufactured to the designer's or end user's precise requirements, they have an almost unlimited number of applications from material handling to loading and unloading of machines, to arc and spot welding. They can also have lasers mounted on them to facilitate a number of tasks, are available in different types – including gantry, four- and six-axis, cleanroom, heat-resistant, and Selective Compliant Assembly (or Articulated) Robot Arm or SCARA robots that are ideal for confined operations – and, in the case of standard or shelf-mounted robots and heavy-duty versions, can be fixed to the floor or ceiling. Moreover, the modular structure of most robots enables them to be easily and quickly reconfigured for different operations. There are of course drawbacks to such technology – principally the fact that robots are not easy machines to use owing to their kinematics, and this is the main reason their greatest application in the automotive industry is for single, repetitive tasks and not complex, multiple operations. Robotics also requires particular ergonomics and specifications that may be hazardous to users. The manufacturers provide guidance for health and safety procedures, correct mounting, and maximum carrying capacity or payload of the robots. These issues may prove prohibitive when considering such industrial processes to be integrated into the fabrication of architectural designs. However, as an emerging mode of translating data to fabricate cutting-edge and highly complex designs, robotics provides fertile ground for greater exploration.

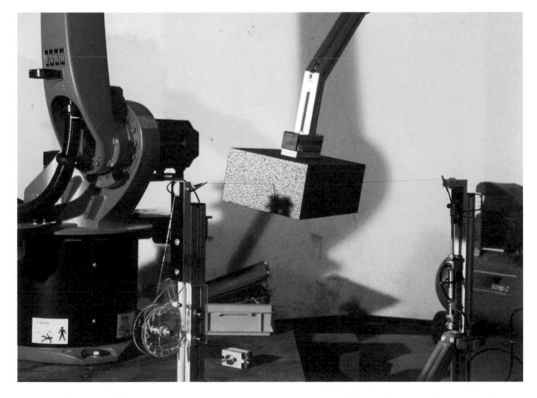

Robots may be used to carry out a sophisticated series of manoeuvres and operations, as illustrated in this example where a robotic arm has lifted, swung, then held a foam block in relation to a hot-wire cutter to enable a precise geometry to be cut from it.

Case study Robotic experimentation and materiality

Supermanoeuvre and Matter Design – wavePavilion, 2010, and additive foam research, 2009.

Dave Pigram of Supermanoeuvre and Wes McGee of Matter Design have collaborated on developing custom software for robotic fabrication for several years. Key to their explorations is the consideration of the material as an intelligent third party in the design process. By using algorithms to directly control the fabrication processes and subsequently reintegrating data from the material's behaviour, they have developed a feedback loop between the digital and material.

While developing robotic fabrication protocols for the wavePavilion, by macdowell. tomova, the architects designed and produced a CNC rod-bending device that operates in conjunction with a multi-use 7-axis robotic arm to shape the components of the pavilion. A custom script was written to translate the design data from the RhinoScript code into a series of procedures for the robot and the bender.

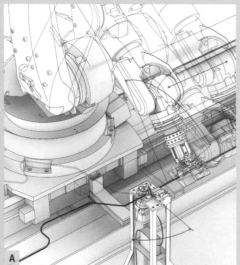

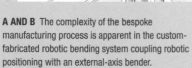

A AND B The complexity of the bespoke manufacturing process is apparent in the custom-fabricated robotic bending system coupling robotic positioning with an external-axis bender.

C Once the tooling of this process is developed, the fabrication of components may be implemented by cold forming to bend the steel tubes.

D The completed pavilion constructed at the University of Michigan's Taubman College of Architecture and Urban Planning, fabricated from more than 1km of 6.35mm (¼ in) diameter steel rod and over 6m x 9m and 4.5m high.

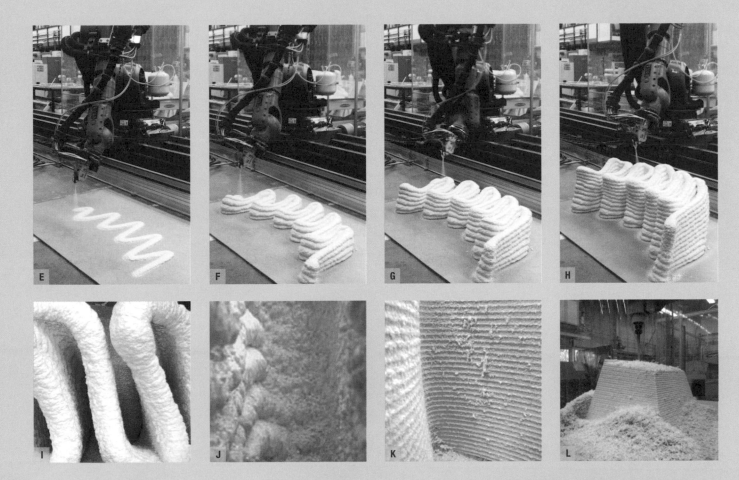

This research into additive foam to make full-size polyethelene foam wall prototypes seeks to respond to the need to consider material and structural logic in relation to form and scale. By integrating robotics to behave as large 3D printers, the potential of the additive process at the scale of building becomes evident. The process is begun by the robot translating a target form into a series of volumetric continuous lines which are machine paths informed by the feed rate and volume of the foam. To be successful, the process has to understand and account for the foam's expansion rate otherwise it is predisposed to distort unpredictably and even collapse. While typical 3D printing machines employ only 3 axes of motion, using a multi-axis robot refines the process of sequential layering by allowing the addition of foam from any angle. This lends more flexibility to the staging of additions and because the foam is more capable of withstanding bending and tension, a better choreographed and considered formal development is possible. The process suggests material mutability, where it might be adapted to other material methods that incur a material phase shift from liquid to solid such as concrete pouring.

E TO H For this research project, the final product of additive foam lends itself to further refinement through the process of milling. After the rough formal volume is achieved, a second pass using a spindle tool allows the subtractive smoothing of the surface. This hybridized process is a method capable of realizing almost any conceivable form.

I TO M The applications for additive foam in architecture are potentially broad: as a mode of realizing large scale form at a reasonable cost, but also as a means to create another end, whereby the foam might be used as temporary formwork in the fabrication and construction sequencing of another production.

Case study Robotic fabrication of architecture
Gramazio & Kohler – Façade of Gantenbein Vineyard, Fläsch, 2006.

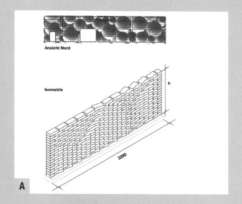

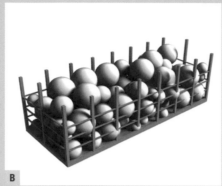

This project developed a non-standardized brick façade for an extension to a Swiss vineyard. The initial design proposed a simple concrete skeleton filled with bricks: the masonry acts as a temperature buffer and filters sunlight to the sensitive fermentation room behind. The bricks are offset, so that daylight penetrates the hall through the gaps between them; direct sunlight is excluded. Polycarbonate panels are mounted inside to protect against wind. On the upper floor, the bricks form the roof-terrace balustrade.

The robotic production method, developed at ETH Zurich, enabled the designers to lay all 20,000 bricks precisely according to programmed parameters – at the required angle and exact, prescribed intervals. This gave each wall the desired light and air permeability, while creating a pattern that covers the entire building. According to the angle at which they are set, the individual bricks reflect light differently and thus take on varying degrees of lightness. Similarly to pixels on a computer screen, they constitute a distinctive image and thus communicate the vineyard's identity. Here, however, there is a dramatic play between plasticity, depth and colour, dependent on the viewer's position and the angle of the sun.

A To create the façade, a generative design process was developed, interpreting the frame construction as a 'basket' and filling it with abstract, oversized 'grapes' of varying diameters. Gravity was digitally simulated to make the grapes fall into this virtual basket until closely packed.

B The result was then viewed from all sides, and the digital image data transferred to the rotation of the individual bricks. However, the architectural implications of this brick façade are more elaborate and diverse than those of a two-dimensional image.

C Robotic production of the wall elements required a complex series of movements to facilitate the correct geometry of each panel.

D In addition to arranging the units the robot also applied bonding agent to each brick in the 400m² façade, according to an automated process developed by the designers to accelerate the manufacturing process. Because each brick has a different rotation, every one had a different and unique overlap with the brick below and above.

E Once the bonding agent had been applied, the bricks were assembled, with the programmed data informing the robot's manoeuvres. Load tests performed on the first manufactured elements revealed that the bonding agent was so structurally effective that the reinforcement normally required for conventional prefabricated walls was unnecessary.

F Because construction was already quite advanced, there was only three months before assembly on site. This made manufacturing the 72 façade elements a challenge, both technologically and time-wise. As the robot could be driven directly by the design data, without the need for additional drawings, the design of the façade was developed up to the last minute before starting production.

G The wall elements were manufactured as a pilot project in research facilities at ETH Zurich, transported by lorry to the construction site and craned into place.

H Installation of the wall panels within the concrete frame on site.

I Internal façade effect, illustrating the 'grapes' and their composition along the wall length.

J External appearance, showing the fine grain and variations of the pattern produced across the individually positioned bricks.

K Joints between the bricks were left open to create transparency and allow daylight to filter inside. To make the pattern discernible from the interior, the bricks were laid as close together as possible so that the gap at full deflection was nearly closed. This produced a maximum contrast between open and closed joints, and allowed light to model the interior walls poetically.

L To the human eye, able to detect the finest difference in colour and lightness, the subtle deflection of the bricks creates an appearance and plasticity that constantly changes along with the movement of the observer and the sun over the course of the day.

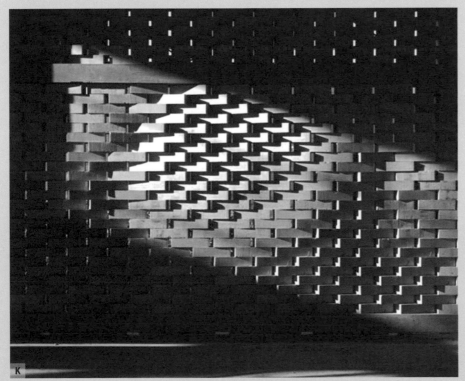

PART 3 STRATEGIES

1. Introduction

Having discussed the range of digital design tools and fabrication techniques available to the architectural designer, it is now time to examine *how* and *why* these may be brought together to provide a strategic approach. Therefore, this section will discuss in more detail how digitally controlled manufacturing processes can be used as both generative and representational tools, and applied to develop intelligent systems for the designer. By comparison with the previous section, we will now focus on the strategic implementation of tools and techniques that enable the generated design and integrated fabrication methods to be maximized for architecture. Key terminology will be presented and defined along with the basic theory behind the different system approaches. Like any design medium, digital making has its own set of possibilities and constraints. The potential to bridge the gap between simulation and construction affords designers access to previously unchartered territory between design and making. The advantages of different techniques, alongside their implications and limitations on modes of inquiry, will be described in order to allow readers to optimize their design methodologies and creative practice. This section will seek to contextualize the application of different techniques in an interdisciplinary manner.

The complexity of architectural-design tasks for which robotics may be used is still an area of experimentation and research rather than widespread practice. Sophisticated arrangements of standard components or the fabrication of non-standard elements are the primary applications of this technology at present.

Left
A key aspect with digital technologies is that practitioners reconsider the way in which they design, both at a conceptual level and with respect to the components used to construct their ideas – see these non-standard 'bricks', which have been intricately laser cut to connect together.

Right
It is important to remember that the design data *is* the construction data, so to achieve the most from these techniques it is important for designers to embrace a holistic understanding of geometry, fabrication techniques and material properties.

Below
Innovative contemporary architecture often absorbs the digital workflow as an integral loop within its design process, providing material and spatial effects that may belie the sophistication and subtleties incorporated into the design – whilst others (as here) reveal their methods in a more explicit manner.

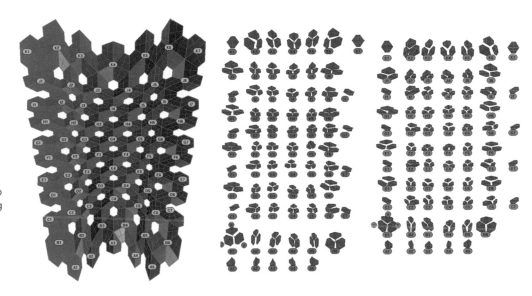

2. Non-linearity and indeterminacy

By now, it will be evident that digital technologies have been transformative in the design process of architecture and present a number of new paradigms for generating and fabricating creative ideas. Core to these changes in the behaviour and approach of the designer using such technologies are the notions of 'indeterminancy' and 'non-linearity'. In this book's first section, we encountered the concept of 'emergence' through the process of morphogenesis, and how this characteristic is being embraced by some designers seeking to develop sophisticated, though not necessarily predictable, results. Because of the willing acceptance by these designers of this unknown nature and its respective outcomes, exciting, unforeseeable and novel concept developments become manifest. The determinism previously endemic in traditional design methods has, through engagement with digital technologies, given way to a 'release' analogous to the creative mental leaps a designer experiences. However, this does not presage a completely random and uncontrollable approach. Instead, what is being developed may be referred to as 'precise indeterminancy'. Seemingly contradictory, this term describes a design process that allows a generative system to run independently but within clearly defined rules or constraints specified by the designer via the information entered into the system. As a direct result of this type of system, the designer's behaviour shifts from 'maker' to 'editor' as preferences are used to decide which emergent forms are appropriate in relation to the desired technical criteria. If this sounds disconnected and clinical, then we might consider Branko Kolarevic's description: 'The generative role of new digital techniques is accomplished through the designer's simultaneous interpretation and manipulation of a computational construct in a complex discourse that is continuously reconstituting itself – a "self-reflexive" discourse in which graphics actively shape the designer's thinking process.'[1]

Digital technologies therefore provide dynamic, critical and analytical modes of inquiry rather than open-ended, ill-defined and simply explorative tools and techniques. The process of form finding intrinsic to this approach reflects the inherently non-linear nature of such design systems as they search through multiple variations. Such methods are not cumulative in the conventional sense, nor are they easily discernible through their various components since they are directed by a complex set of relations and mutual dependencies.

1. Kolarevic, B. [ed.] (2003) *Architecture in the Digital Age: Design and Manufacturing.* Spon Press, p.42.

Digital making does not merely provide an expanded 'toolkit' for architects, but may represent a complete methodological approach to practice. The highly innovative, engaging projects by Studio Gang Architects, such as their design for South Pond at Lincoln Park Zoo in Chicago, demonstrate the capability of a digital approach and its application. Inspired by tortoise shells, the pavilion has a laminated structure of prefabricated, bent-wood members and a series of interconnected fibreglass pods that provide surface curvature.

3. Digital tooling

In this book so far, we have encountered a wide range of digital design and fabrication approaches that may enhance or replace traditional aspects of the architectural design process. For the inexperienced designer these are valuable routes into the world of digital technologies, as they afford the integration of new modes of inquiry with more familiar ones. However, in order to explore the deeper potentialities of digital design and making it is helpful to consider some key aspects in relation to the designer's intentions. This is particularly relevant in CAD/CAM processes since the choice of fabrication explicitly and implicitly informs design ideas. With this in mind, it is useful to consider the most appropriate application at the very beginning of the design process. As we shall see, there are a number of key ways of integrating digital technologies to achieve the desired results. This process is sometimes referred to as 'tooling', defined as 'the provision and setting up of tools for e.g. a machining process.'[2] This definition is pertinent to digital fabrication, and forms the basis of the perspective advocated by Aranda and Lasch in their influential 2006 publication, *Tooling*. Rather than viewing design tools and fabrication techniques as separate stages in a digital workflow, tooling acknowledges the interdependency of these modes, and 'traces the movement between this state of potential and manifest architecture. This movement, or movements, occurs in a dynamic space of interchange where the algorithms and the evolving diversity of figures that crystallize from them are in constant communication and formation with external pressures.'[3] This section will therefore describe the tooling processes most frequently implemented by architectural designers, often leading towards highly innovative and cutting-edge projects through their inquiries. These approaches are:

- Contouring
- Folding
- Forming
- Sectioning
- Tiling

2. *The Chambers Dictionary*. Chambers Harrap, 2001.

3. Aranda, B. & Lasch, C. (2006) *Tooling*. Pamphlet Architecture no. 27. Princeton Architectural Press, p.9.

By reconnecting architects to the material aspect of their work through direct engagement with full-size prototypes, digital making has allowed a new generation of designers to explore ideas in direct correlation to their fabrication techniques. West 8 work with 1:1 prototypes as an intrinsic part of their design practice. Their development of large-scale masterplanning, urban-design and landscape strategies is balanced by the investigation of elements at the human scale of the user. In the design for the Leidsche Rijn Park, Vieuten, the office used CNC milling to produce a full-size prototype of a bridge balustrade panel. This enabled the pattern, colour and other design features to be evaluated prior to casting in metal.

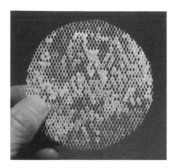

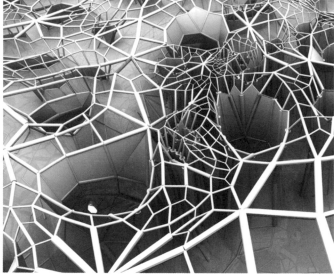

GEOtube is a proposed high-rise tower in Dubai. Designed by Faulders Studio, it features an open structure and exposed-membrane skin, its vertical planes becoming misted with local saltwater owing to an external vascular water system. As a result, the visible surfaces have an ongoing uniform growth of salt-crystal deposits; the building's skin is 'grown' rather than constructed, and is in 'continual formation' rather than complete. In addition to the visual transformation from transparent veil to white plane, the salt crystals produce air saturated with negative ions that may address the considerable amount of positive ions produced by atmospheric pollution. The physical mesh experiments and CAD visualizations illustrate the intended development of the tower's surfaces.

STEP BY STEP ROBOTIC ASSEMBLY

For the Designers Saturday project at Langenthal, Gramazio & Kohler collaborated with industrial design students from FHNW, Switzerland, to produce an intervention. The structural design concept was initially developed during a workshop at the Smart Geometry Conference 2010 in Barcelona, and subsequently applied in this project for the first time at a larger scale.

1 Each polystyrene module is individually cut within a non-standard fabrication process, using an industrial robot and a hot-wire machine.

2 The design comprises 1,022 non-standard polystyrene modules, which are assembled into a large-scale mesh structure.

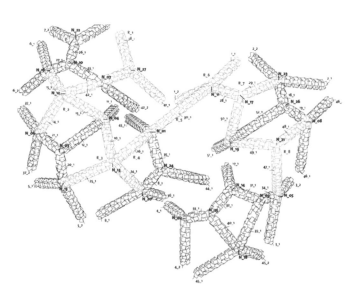

3 The overall geometry of the mesh is based on a digitally simulated hanging-chain model that allows an optimal force flow within the structure. It thus enables the delicate design of each of the individual arches, which are manually assembled.

4 The polystyrene modules spiral along the single arches. The structural interlocking of the modules supports the stability of the overall structure and enables the precise placement of each without further technical support.

STEP BY STEP DIGITAL SCRIPTING AND MAKING

The Natural Code pavilion project by Tim Marjot was developed from an initial concept related to Fibonacci curves and the potential of spiral geometry. Using the project to learn the potential of generative design, Marjot used a variety of digital design and fabrication methods to explore his ideas and their potential implementation.

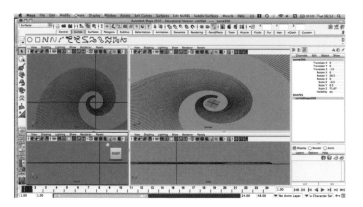

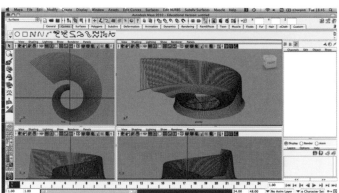

1 Initial experiments with NURB Curves using Autodesk MAYA and MEL Script. The data in the 'Make Rib' section iterates the production of a curve with a number of points located along it, whose location determines the curve's form; in this case, it creates a bench. This form is then repeated, each time scaled by 1.01.

2 The final script incorporates the creation of a wall, enclosing the environment and creating an intimate, sheltered space. The seat also gradually increases in height as it spirals round. This allows people at the back to see past the bench for presentations, and a variety of bench heights for the broad age range that will be using the environment.

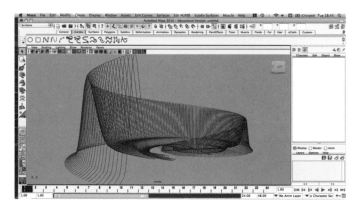

3 Single-window view of final script, illustrating curvilinear geometry formed by ribs set along spiral path.

4 Design data is taken from the scripted CAD model and used to inform a laser cutter. This produces the ribs from card in order to appreciate the design's physical aspects at a small scale.

5 Photomontage of model, showing design in context, to communicate implications and impact of the pavilion to the client.

Case study Responsive digital making

sixteen*(makers) – Residency, Kielder Water and Forest Park, Northumberland, 2003–7.

Upon appointment, the designers were informed that no architectural outcome was expected but that a role for architecture in Kielder should be explored. There were two key aspects to the project. First, to explore difference in micro-environments across the territory in order to inform strategies for future architectural interventions. Second, to develop a method of designing architecture within a context in a continual state of change. The body of work as a whole involves the interdependent practices of design through representation and design through making, and occupies the increasingly interconnected worlds of digital and analogue design.

A Survey probes were designed to act as dual monitors and responsive objects. Common to many architectural constructs, the probes were initially designed by drawing – in this case as a 3D CAD model. As a property of the software in which it was designed, this 'original' model was animated prior to manufacture in response to an input of environmental (real) data gathered on site. Thus, pre-manufacture a preview of how they might behave was ascertained. As a digital preview, this performance was a simulation, in other words an 'idealized' response that relied on the capability of the controlling software to interpret 'real' data.

B Once the design was appropriately determined, laser-cut parts were fabricated for the survey probes.

C The precision of the digital manufacturing process enabled the steel components to be assembled manually.

D Installed on site, the probes' dynamic behaviour, activated by the micro-environment, was captured by an array of high-resolution digital cameras programmed to record at regular intervals.

E The majority of related research in 'evolutionary' design processes focuses on the role of computational representation. Using feedback loops between real and digital, this project places equivalent status upon realization and representation – and is seen as a novel investigation within this field.

F The captured visual data was later developed to generate three-dimensional outline models via digital photogrammetry software. The resulting 3D outline models were superimposed upon time-lapse footage of the probes, generating a digital–analogue composite.

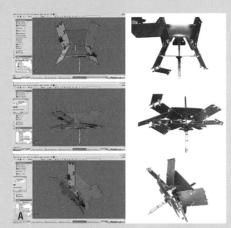

Case study Hybrid techniques for interactive architecture
NOX – D-Tower, Doetinchem, 1999–2004.

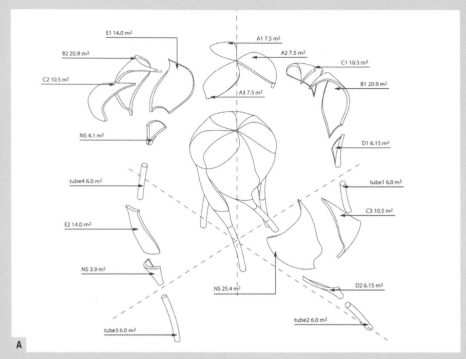

E1 14.0 m²

B2 20.9 m²

A1 7.5 m²

A2 7.5 m²

C2 10.5 m²

C1 10.5 m²

B1 20.9 m²

A3 7.5 m²

NS 4.1 m²

D1 6.15 m²

tube4 6.0 m²

tube1 6.0 m²

C3 10.5 m²

E2 14.0 m²

NS 3.9 m²

NS 25.4 m²

D2 6.15 m²

tube2 6.0 m²

tube3 6.0 m²

A

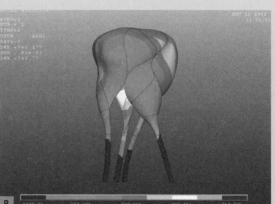

B

C

The D-Tower is a hybrid of different media, wherein architecture becomes part of a larger interactive system of relationships. The project comprises a physical structure (the tower), a questionnaire and a website. All three are related to one another. The tower is a 12m-high structure, similar to a Gothic vault where columns and surfaces share a continuum. It connects to a website, which visualizes the inhabitant's response to a questionnaire via four colours. Its complex geometry is developed to echo a beating human heart. Each evening, the computer concludes from the responses which emotion is most intensely felt that day and lights the D-tower in the corresponding colour.

A The D-Tower comprises 19 separate panels, as illustrated by the assembly schematic above.

B Analysis software enables the designer to understand the loading and stress implications of the design, and adjust the geometry if necessary.

C A CNC milling machine is used to cut expanded polystyrene blocks, which are combined to form moulds for different panels.

D Each mould is assembled using CNC-cut blocks, as shown above.

E The panels are made from glass-reinforced epoxy (GRE), with the moulds being laminated to produce the complex curvilinear panel designs.

D

E

F, G, H, I, J AND K Underneath, daytime and chromatic night-time views of the final design. For more details and real-time streaming of the project see: www.d-teen.nl

Case study A performative façade
Joanna Szulda – The Soft and Furry Façade, 2010.

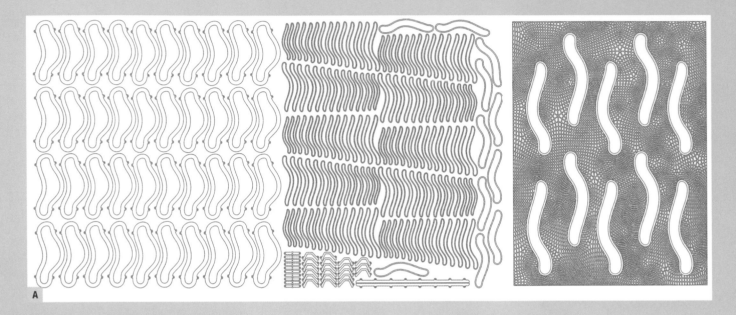

A

The examination of this façade through tests simulating external environment effects on its components proves its powerful sensual and emotional effects on the observer. The design of the façade module is no rootless object, but a skin of topographic construction engaged with its Santa Monica beach site. It derives inspiration from the hidden features of the building's urban setting, and the organic fabric of barnacles attached to the pier's pillars. Using contemporary CAD techniques and CAM technologies, the project explores multidimensional programmatic components – its surfaces, patterns, and spatial geometries created within the Soft and Furry Façade. The prototype component comprises two external parts: a laser-cut shelter forming the base, and a group of overhanging optical-fibre rods. All together, there are ten components vertically assembled to the prototype wall, manufactured at 1:1 scale. The component is not only an ornament related to the urban context, but an intuitive device. The ornamental patterns are an essential tool for architectural articulation. They evoke emotion, communication with the user (often on a subconscious level, demanding focused attention) and they convey almost immediately intuitive information about the space. Finally, they interact with environmental conditions – such as light, wind or humidity – to introduce sensual, responsive behaviour to the user.

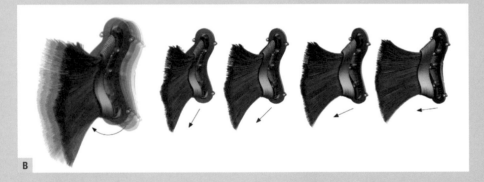

B

A 2D laser-cut drawings.

B Axonometric diagram of exploded component.

C Sequence of rotating component

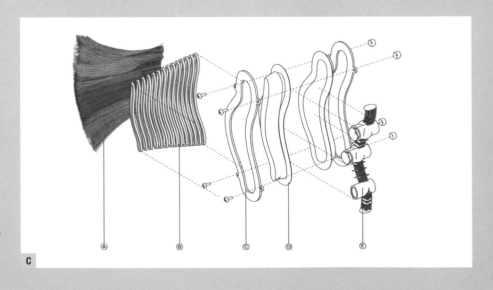

C

The base comprises 14 medium-density fibreboard laser-cut forms, gradually scaled down and arranged one on top of another. The optical-fibre rods are attached to the vacuum-formed structure, and artificially brighten from the inside to project light on the outside of the component. The prototype is made at 1:1 scale. The external MDF element has the dimensions 260mm x 25mm x 45mm, while the 250 optical-fibre rods are 1mm in diameter. The rods are 250mm long in total, of which 160mm are visible on the outside. The internal section of the component comprises two vacuum-formed elements, which engage the electrical mechanism to light the rods. The prototype wall is 550mm wide and 750mm long. Ten components are vertically assembled on the external envelope, made of plywood board. The internal part of each ornament (the vacuum-formed piece) is held behind the outer envelope by a pair of metal rods, which together form a frame with the possibility of moving to the left and right.

D Prototype model of the 'performing' component.

E AND F Front and rear views of the prototype wall.

G The final installation, illustrating the performative ornamental components of the design.

4. Contouring

Many of the materials used in the production of architecture are processed in or from a sheet format. Whilst they may have radically varying properties – most obviously with respect to colour, texture and thickness – these are essentially planar elements. Contouring changes this physical materiality by using an incremental subtractive technique, not dissimilar to carving, to provide three-dimensional features from what is ostensibly a 'flat' sheet material. Carving, of course, is a long-established technique of working with materials in architecture, principally in stone and wood in a period that stretches back to ancient civilizations. The main difference between the two processes lies in the nature of the tooling in each method. Carving is traditionally a manual, crafts-based skill, which has experienced considerable decline in the preceding century of industrial standardization and manufacturing. This situation has altered dramatically through the use of digital fabrication, which offers the possibility of highly articulated and intricately patterned components. Specifically, the implementation of CNC milling and routing enables the designer to systematically remove material through a series of carvings or contours. In contrast to the manual approach, CNC methods are capable of quickly producing a greater number of either non-standard or repetitive elements – and the level of detail in each approach may be comparable. Typical materials used with this process are wood and foams, although metals may also be used.

The tooling opportunities with contouring facilitate a clear dialogue between the digital design information and the making process. However, the subtractive nature of CNC milling and routing renders this technique time-consuming and demanding of considerable amounts of material. This is because the waste material removed to produce the desired contoured surface or component may, firstly, be significant in volumetric terms and, secondly, has been machined with a high level of detail in order to leave the equally sophisticated product behind. It is important to understand the implications of these factors in relation to time and cost in order to ensure that this is the most suitable method of digital fabrication. The process of contouring has enabled architects to achieve highly imaginative effects from traditional materials, by articulating their properties in an effective and transformative manner.

Contouring is readily achieved using CNC routing and milling processes, and may extend surface characteristics by incorporating geometrical variation and complexity into otherwise planar materials. These images show the production of an undulating panel for use in dECOi/Mark Goulthorpe's design for One Main. To see how this element was incorporated into the final design, refer to pages 136–8.

STEP BY STEP CONTOURING

This project uses the contouring of material blocks to create modular components that are adaptable in use and arrangement. Designed and completed by Faulders Studio for the Berkeley Art Museum and Pacific Film Archive, BAMscape is a shaped assembly of 150 individual curved modules. Each was fabricated using digital methods, which enabled efficient production directly from CAD drawings as well as considerable variation (all the contours are unique).

1 Polystyrene blocks are cut with a hotwire cutter in the first stage of the CNC-cutting process to achieve the individual, contoured geometry.

2 The application of digitally driven manufacturing allows the non-standard elements to be economically viable and easily produced.

3 By cladding in 9mm-thick bendable plywood for the top surfaces and 6mm-thick plywood for the sides, the modules are given a protective coating.

4 The use of polystyrene blocks enables channels for cable routes etc. to be readily incorporated on site; here, the modules await delivery.

5 The resulting footprint of the object is 145m^2 of undulating curves. Visually bold, structurally innovative, kinesthetically engaging – the design communicates a playful inventiveness, allowing users to engage with the space and reconfiguring modules in relation to programmes and events.

Case study Contouring an object

Gramazio & Kohler – mTable, 2002.

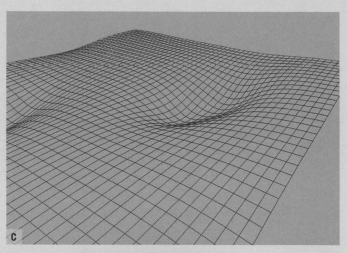

This customizable table series was developed to enable people to design their own table by mobile phone. The mTable is created using contouring processes to sculpt a surface, choosing dimensions, materials and colours. These parameters are directly transmitted to CNC fabrication for the production of each bespoke table.

A AND B In the first stage of the process, the user downloads the mTable application onto a compatible mobile phone.

C The design is then adapted using actions related to pressure, dimension and material before being submitted. The pressure function allows the user to sculpt a smooth landscape for the table surface using one of seven deformers.

D The bespoke design-data order is transmitted directly to the manufacturer, where CNC milling contours the table.

E The contouring process is highly accurate and facilitated by the use of a special bit attached to the machine head, which produces a smooth motion and effect.

F Each unique mTable is shipped, between 8 and 12 weeks later, to the designer/customer. This results in a wealth of variations within a limited number of parameters.

G, H AND I The mass-customization process afforded by digital design and fabrication techniques is utilized here to offer the role of designer to the customer/end user. For more information on this project see: www.mshape.com

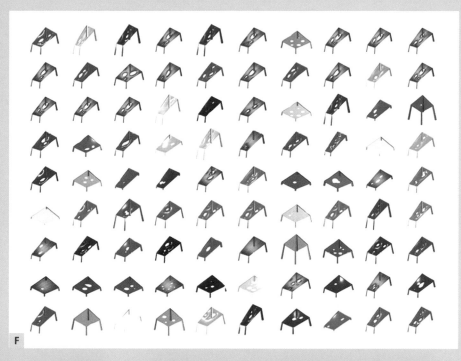

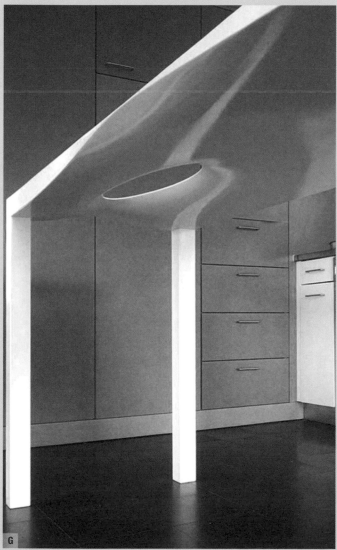

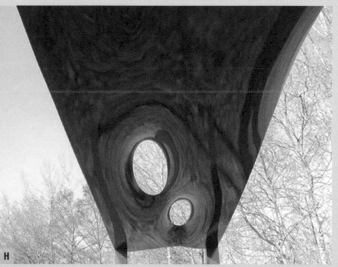

Case study Contouring to fabricate a mould

AL_ A – Spencer Dock Bridge, Dublin, 2006–9.

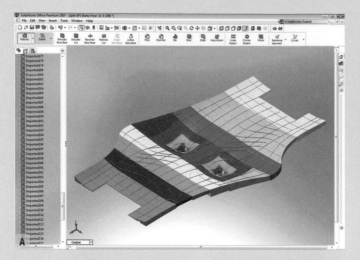

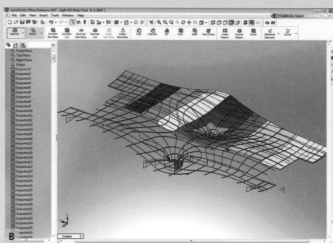

This 40m-span bridge with its fluid lines and undulating concrete surface takes trams, traffic and pedestrians across the Royal Canal. Its deck edges peel down to reveal a space for pedestrians to pause and take in views of the dock and adjacent Linear Park. The bridge's underside merges with its piers in a single movement, with joint lines in the concrete designed to accentuate the form's geometry. The concrete finish provides high visibility against the dark water, and at night the structure is vibrantly lit from below, underlining its fluid form. The bridge's proportions are unusual, and the design exploits these by treating it as a piece of landscaping. The soft geometry and asymmetry create a piece of infrastructure that resolves tensions between form and function.

A The geometry was remodelled in Solidworks to generate EPS moulds and control assembly tolerance.

B View showing cut-away of EPS block model and dummy rebate network.

C Fabricating directly from the 3D parametric models provided a high degree of control over the geometry. The formwork was manufactured in high-density EPS foam machined on a 5-axis router.

D The foam was milled in increments of greater surface resolution.

E The formed face was sprayed with three coats of polyurea, and sanded. The finished 3m x 1.25m blocks were then shipped to site.

F The blocks were assembled on a ply falsework deck. Position and accuracy were controlled with a network of tongue-and-groove slots that connected to the soffits of the formwork and a digital total station.

G 10mm spacers were left between the formwork blocks to allow for site adjustment and thermal creep. The joints were then sealed, and dummy rebates and reinforcement mat incorporated.

H AND I This innovative use of CNC-cut polystyrene is to date the largest such application of the material. White limestone was used in the concrete mix to increase visibility and reflect changing water patterns. The concrete edges were precast off site, and incorporate recessed lighting and the stainless-steel balustrade.

Case study Contouring to make continuous surfaces

dECOi/Mark Goulthorpe – One Main, Cambridge, Massachusetts, 2008–9.

This office-refurbishment project rigorously deploys CNC machining of sustainable plywood to demonstrate the versatility and efficiency available using CAD/CAM design–build processes. It displaces the combinatorial logic of ready-made components in favour of a seamless, non-standard protocol of customized fabrication. A formal asethetic emerges from such processes, imbuing the design with a curvilinear continuity at spatial and detail levels. Materially, the design assumes an environmental agenda, using a sustainable, carbon-absorbing raw material (forested spruce), translated efficiently into refined and functional elements via dexterous low-energy digital tooling.

A

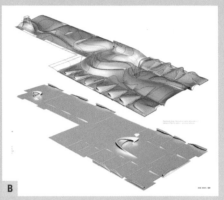

B

C

A Sketch design, suggesting the plastic potential offered by CNC machining of sustainable timber.

B Developed design, showing local plastic deformation of ceiling and floor for spatial or functional definition.

C Developed ceiling form, with procedural scripting processes for generation of millwork files.

D Scripting logic to nest machining files on plywood sheets for direct milling.

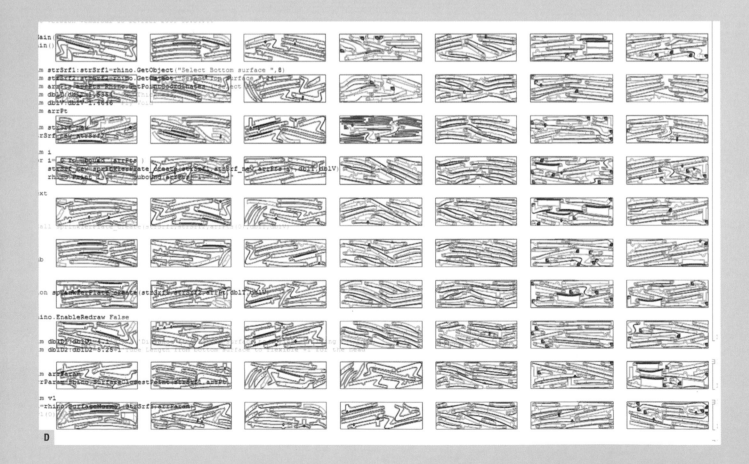

D

E, F AND G Fabrication of secretarial inflection.

H With the exception of the glass, all design components are fabricated as stacked, sectional elements cut from flat plywood sheets by a single 3-axis CNC milling machine. This unitary fabrication method offers a streamlining of the typical multi-trade assembly techniques, with evident economies of labour, materials and logistics. Therefore, despite the formal complexity that such a process entails significant economy is provided via a single fabricator, with a versatile digital tool, being able to execute the entire project.

I Floor 'carpets' prefabricated off site and installed as finished elements.

J Installation of secretarial inflection as a large prefabricated element, minimizing site work.

K, L AND M Milling of mathematical surfaces at end grain of laminated ply.

N Installation of conference table and office desks.

O Finished secretarial desk alloplastically linked to ceiling inflection.

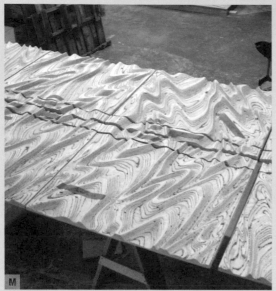

STEP BY STEP CONTOURING MODULAR ELEMENTS

The Landscape Lounge project for the Dutch Embassy in Berlin by ONL uses contouring from high-density foam. These multipurpose objects, designed by an architect and a sculptor, have more than one 'face': owing to parametric design and optimal use of the cutting method, five complementary forms in two and even three directions are cut out of one huge block of 1m x 1.2m x 4m material. The lines of the elements, touching each other, result in a set of stackable objects, usable in various ways. Each of the five elements is different in form, typical of ONL's use of non-standard design to enhance user interaction. Whether used as a high or low table, a seat or a lounge chair, the 'landscape' of elements is varied after each use so that a different configuration is left/awaiting each time.

1 3D digital model of molecular element.

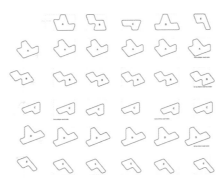
2 Parametric iterations of different modules.

3 CAD/CAM interface, showing design data sent to CNC machine to be contoured from a block.

4 Modular element is removed from its original block.

5 Completed component, showing complex geometry.

6 Variations of modular blocks.

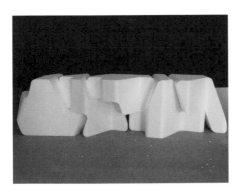
7 Stacking potential offers myriad possibilities.

8 Once coated to protect the foam, the elements may be used in a range of different spaces, such as interiors ...

9 ... or positioned, for greater adaption by users, outside.

5. Folding

A much more familiar process of developing two-dimensional surfaces into three-dimensional forms is that of folding. In addition to articulating flat sheet materials into formal propositions, folding has rich potential for defining structural geometry. Through folding, the self-supporting effective span and rigidity of sheet materials may increase substantially, offering further design developments. In comparison to contouring, folding is very economical in material terms. Already an engaging method of exploring design ideas at various scales, digital fabrication has afforded even further experimentation with this material operation. Perhaps the most immediate characteristic of folding is the continuity of space, surface and form it provides, enabling a fluidity distinct from most other tooling methods. It is possible to understand folding not simply as a representational approach offering direct, dynamic – i.e. continuous – relationships between design elements, but also as a generative technique that, through exploration of a surface's features and how these may be further nuanced, may prove valuable to the designer. Whilst the material operation may seem relatively finite when using traditional methods, digital

technologies enable the calculation and setting out of complex fold patterns, furnishing the practitioner with a greater spectrum of design options. As a translation process, converting two-dimensional surface into three-dimensional modulated form, folding already has an extensive history in product design and other creative disciplines. However, digital-fabrication technology readily allows the designer to shift from a scale model to full-size spatial prototypes and installations, which permit the architectural qualities of design ideas to be not only explored but also directly experienced.

The apparently limitless potential of folding as a tooling strategy has, as with all the other approaches described in this section, been assisted by digital design software, including a number of programs with specific functions within their interfaces that convert free-form surfaces into unfolded pattern sheets ready for digital fabrication. The data for these unfolded sheets is usually used with cutting machines – particularly laser cutters, although plasma and water-jet cutters may also be engaged for this process. The advantage of laser cutters is that they can score sheet material rather than cut

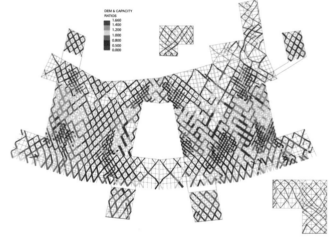

Folding is often an integral feature of many contemporary architectural designs, aided by the ability of computation to fold and unfold designs and analyze different variables. For the China Central Television (CCTV) Headquarters by OMA, two towers lean towards one another and connect in an apparently gravity-defying cantilever (left). The distinctive loop was developed through extensive analysis of structural implications alongside aesthetic considerations, and necessitated digital simulation of the building façade's bracing structure as a composite, unfolded skin (right).

all the way through its thickness, affording folds to be more easily made, whereas other cutters create a series of holes – typically lines of perforations – to assist folding. In material terms, the very act of manipulating the surface through bends, creases and other modulations requires that the intended sheet be flexible in nature, and as a consequence thick paper, sheet metal and plastics are the most commonly used materials – although the latter necessitates heating to become suitably pliable.

Below
The strategy of folding is clearly evident in the articulated exterior of UNStudio's design for the Theatre Agora, Lelystad, which follows the flat, unfolded patterns of the diagrammatic elevations to create a three-dimensional sculptural form. The building's envelope comprises an overlapping multifaceted surface, whose perforations create a kaleidoscopic effect.

Bottom
The logic of folded surfaces continues throughout, and is amplified in the auditorium where it provides both a formal and acoustic strategy.

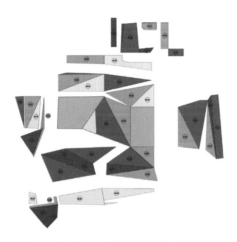

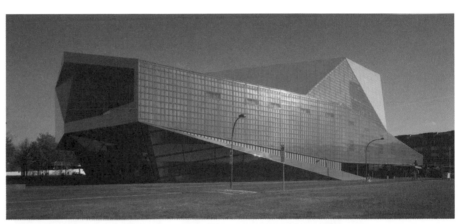

Case study Folding as surface strategy
Reiser + Umemoto – Vector Wall, New York, 2008.

The Vector Wall imagines ways that a simple laser cutter can perforate a flexible or semi-flexible material with multidirectional patterning, reinterpreting the common wall. The project explores the system of laser cutting a standard steel sheet and bending/folding it to create an undulating perforated surface; once cut, a flat steel sheet can form a volumetric, scalable, diaphanous scrim. This flexible wall module can extend from its original 1.2m x 2.4m sheet size into a dimensionally variable panel. Through this approach to laser cutting, a standard material may transcend its dimensions not only in the X and Y axes but also in the Z axis, exponentially increasing the variety of its uses.

Vector Wall illustrates late twentieth-century prefabrication logic taking advantage of new digital design and manufacturing processes. The idea of developing a rigid plane into an independent articulated surface arrived relatively

early in the design process. It developed from an interest in rigid fabric systems as building materials, and migrated towards steel as an efficient medium, exhibiting strength and rigidity while remaining extremely thin. The final size of the piece is a direct result of the prefabrication dimensions of standard steel sheets, as the designers attempted to utilize as much of each sheet as possible. In its final iteration, the design was split into six pieces to conform to cutting beds, transportation and finishing constraints. The pieces were cut, fabricated, individually powder-coated and then bolted together with removable fittings to allow easy transportation, installation and disassembly.

A The design process explored laser-cutting a rigid sheet by prototyping in paper. This enabled a study of volumetric and surface effects, while partially understanding the limited flexibility of the system.

B Once a method for manipulating the surface was established, prototyping in steel was essential in evaluating the effects and failures of the forms responding to the cut pattern in the actual material. The designers worked closely with the laser cutter to determine the thickness and composition of the material, as well as minimum and maximum cut widths, cut lengths and spacing. As such, the entire process of designing included as much, if not more, making and testing as it did planning.

C Essential to the design was the isolation of formal variables in the cut pattern, and the various effects they produced on the resultant surface. The final form combines structural articulation – such as branching, weight distribution and material accumulation – with aesthetic or atmospheric effects, such as variable visibility, porosity/opacity, luminosity and perceived spatial manipulation and material flow.

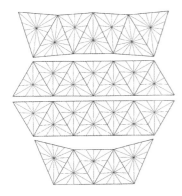

The Starlight Theatre, Rockford, by Studio Gang Architects, incorporates a faceted roof structure whose folding geometry permits the centre sections to open upward, so that each roof panel overlaps its neighbour in a similar manner to flower petals. Replacing an existing outdoor venue, the central theatre space forms an unexpected vertical axis, an observatory to the stars through a kinetic steel-and-timber roof that opens in fair weather.

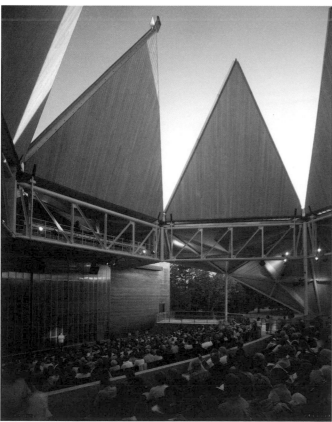

Case study Folding as reconfigurable and interactive installation
sixteen*(makers) – *Blusher*, various locations, 2001.

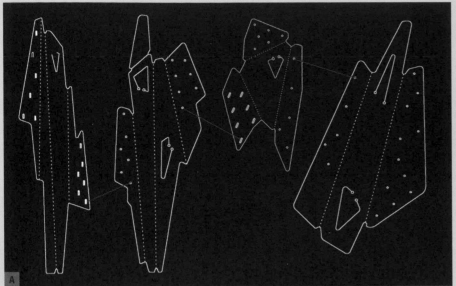

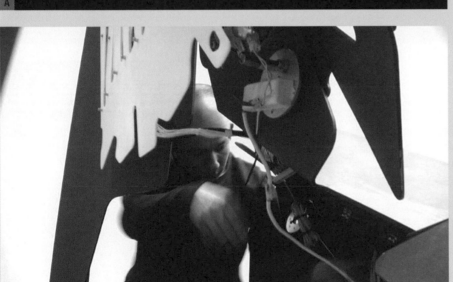

A CAD drawing indicating four of the variably cut steel plates with fold lines demarcated.

B This information then informed the CNC plasma-cutting process.

C The cut components were pressed to achieve the folds, and fabricate three-dimensional pieces from two-dimensional shapes of material.

D The network of sensors, which detect proximity and movement near the installation, were connected to the folded elements.

This practice's interdisciplinary research is primarily developed through the practice of making, with respect to the impact of digital technologies and time-based architecture. Their projects explore the interfaces between craft and manufacturing, utilizing a variety of techniques including CAD/CAM processes and software script writing. Conceived as an adaptive and variable installation, to be set within a number of exhibition spaces, *Blusher* negotiates spatial and temporal relationships between occupants and their environment.

Blusher is effectively a kit of interchangeable elements, allowing assembly at each venue with specific spatial relationships to the site. It comprises three series of components: firstly, a set of 21 variably cut and folded steel plates, capable of interconnecting in several ways; secondly, a network of embedded sensors including proximity sensors, retro-reflective beam breakers and a sonar device; and thirdly, a layered surface of polycarbonate leaves with responsive properties, known as 'feathers'.

E AND F The differential qualities of logged data, once correlated and assessed, allowed fine-grain inferences to be made about movement, direction, density, proximity and occupancy-duration. Subsequently, the data was used to drive the feathers, which fluttered and glowed in various ways.

G AND H The assembled array of steel plates formed structural enclosures, spatial boundaries and 'luring' elements. Embedded within this array, the sensory network monitored immediate and adjacent territories, routes and lines of approach, and logged activity in these zones as data on a microprocessor. Various intensities of 'blush', related to the history of sensory data and live stimuli, were witnessed. As trends began to emerge from the data set, it was possible for *Blusher* to make behaviour predictions with greater certainty and respond with increasing confidence. The research demonstrates how the use of historical data in relation to real-time activity allows systems to extend beyond being merely reflexive to being adaptive.

Case study Folded surfaces as articulated roof and landscape

EMERGENT/Tom Wiscombe – MoMA/P.S.1 Urban Beach, Queens, New York, 2003.

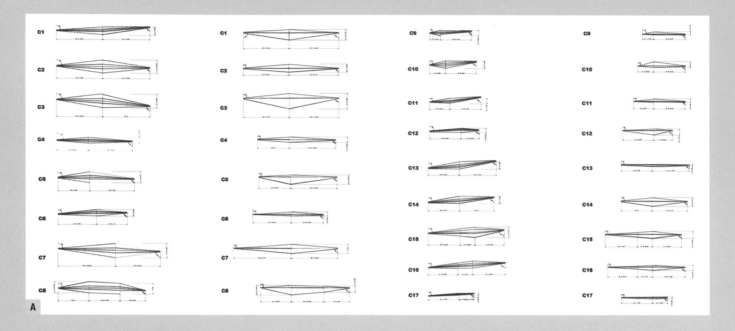

A

The P.S.1 Urban Beach, realized in the PS1 Contemporary Art Center courtyard, was based on two distinct but interrelated systems: the Cellular Roof and the Leisure Landscape. The landscape integrates various programmatic elements such as long lap pools, furniture for sitting and lounging, and promenade catwalks at different heights. Also, at key points the landscape begins to adapt into structural supports for the roof. These behaviours are integrated into a coherent 'gradient' of use, spilling out rhizomatically into the courtyard, resolving the space into microclimates and passageways.

A The Cellular Roof necessitated creating a long-span structure through a non-hierarchical structural patterning of distinct, but interlaced, units, or 'cells'. The location and geometry of each cell was determined by local shading requirements, by its required shear and moment reactions, and by the behaviour of neighbouring cells.

B The expanded aluminium-skin cladding was generated using minimal surface geometry, primarily conoidal and parabolic surfaces. These were generated by 'lofting' straight-line segments with parabolas or rotated-line segments, creating a slight warp to each panel. This warping, and the associated vaulting, stiffened the panels against sagging. The warping was adopted in the meshwork of the material itself, and therefore the panels could still be unfolded flat and water-jet cut for economical manufacture.

C One of the goals of this project was to integrate issues of fabrication and erection into the design process. As a temporary-event roof needing to be designed, manufactured and installed in just two months, the project was forced to jump directly from conceptual design to shop drawings – a feat made possible by digital-fabrication techniques. The key was to avoid designing a fixed shape and concentrate on creating a controlled geometrical logic which could adapt easily to changes in structural stresses, scope, programme and other conditions.

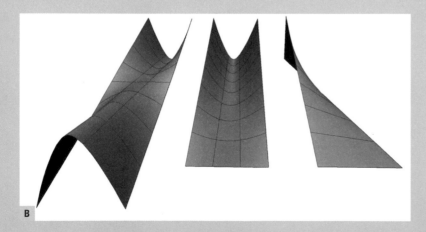

B

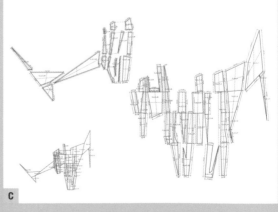

C

D The interconnected cells operated in alliance, enabling large, clear spans and forming a structural 'ecology'. A crenellated second skin wraps these elements into a unified shade structure. At night, however, this provisional body transforms back into an atmospheric light-emitting 'swarm', characterized by its cellularity.

E Urban Beach installation complete and in use.

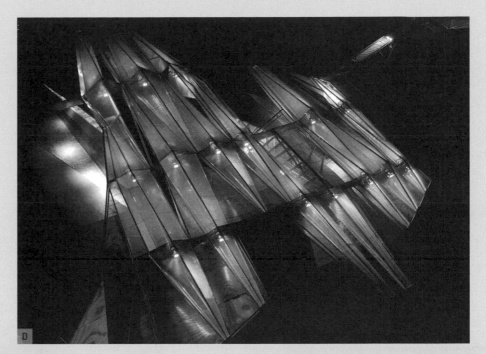

6. Forming

Formative processes have been discussed earlier, but the procedure of forming is relevant again here since it requires a particular approach in relation to the digital technologies that enable it. Forming is tooling through the generation of components from a mould or form, and is most readily applied for the mass production of consumer products. It has been used to make such architectural elements as façade panels, detail components and other hardware. On site, forming is a long-established process for producing precast structural columns and beams, walls, panels or even whole zones of the building such as circulation cores. Digital fabrication approaches the method in a similar manner, requiring a mould or form which is usually created via CNC milling but occasionally uses rapid-prototyping techniques. The forming process produces positive and negative moulds, also referred to as 'male' and 'female'. Positive moulds are used for thermo- and vacuum moulding, whilst negative moulds may also facilitate casting and injection moulding. Both types afford metal stamping and other comparable methods. Forming is an effective and relatively economical method of making a significant number of components, and as a result it is typical for a great deal of effort, time and cost to be spent in the fabrication of the moulds. The forming process has considerable potential for architectural design, since it may be utilized with a variety of materials and be easily integrated with traditional and digital modes of making. Perhaps to an even greater degree than with folding, the key advantages of this approach relate to full-size fabrication, which makes it an effective bridge between digital design and production.

Below
Forming is a key way of making curvilinear elements. The size and shape of each part is typically constrained by the limits of the mould that may be produced by the CNC machine. This lighting feature by Greg Lynn FORM demonstrates the numerous sections needed for fabrication. Note also the incorporation of a lip around the edge of each part to facilitate connection.

Bottom right
Using CNC routing and milling to create complex formwork for the fabrication of components is a primary method employed by architects, as illustrated by this scale prototype panel for the interior of the CocoonClub designed by 3deluxe.

A

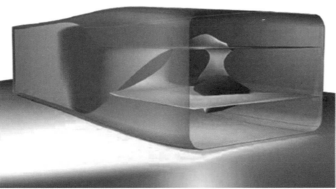

UNStudio's design for the Music Theatre in Graz shows the use of forming to provide the fluid geometry of the 3D digital model. The building is structured to combine a unit-based volume – the theatre's 'black box' – and a series of movement-based volumes such as the foyer and public circulation. Because this organizing principle is made constructive, a fluent internal spatial arrangement is achieved. The free-flowing foyer space is made possible by a spiralling constructive element that connects the entrance to the auditorium and to the music rooms above, thus welding together 'with a twist' the three levels of this side of the building.

A 3D digital model, illustrating internal fluidity of circulation and foyer spaces.

B The exterior, its translucent façade exposing the internal geometry.

C 3D 'twist', made using complex formwork to produce the desired flow of curvilinear concrete.

D The ribbon of 'flowing' concrete glides through the triple-height space.

E Additional materials and colour are used selectively to further nuance the sweeping geometry and emphasize its sculptural qualities.

B

C

D

E

STEP BY STEP FORMING AND CASTING

The integration of digital-fabrication technologies for moulding and casting complex curved forms is a growing area of experimentation. In this example of a scaled bronze version of the Blue Gallery by dECOi/Mark Goulthorpe, the production of the object mirrored the building process.

1 The basic form of the curved surfaces, cut as 2D ply sections, are laminated together and sanded to produce a 'positive' form for the sand/resin mould.

2 The moulding process, where a liquid sets in a curvilinear mould, is in fact a scaled-down version of the typical techniques of the composite industry, where resins reinforced by fibre mats are cast in numeric command milled moulds.

3 The casting process in bronze, yielding a sensual and heavily plastic form which was subject to grinding to smooth its edges and then received a blue-grey patina. This process alerted the designers to the potential for non-standard components and spaces to be moulded in this manner, which fed into the casting of components in future projects.

STEP BY STEP FORMING AS EXPLORATIVE PROCESS

This series of models, both digital and physical, was made by Barkow Leibinger to investigate possible iterations of a spaceframe for a building façade. The design development explored different geometric configurations that would provide structural stability.

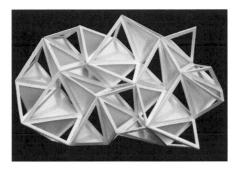

1 Early digital model of double 'mesh' skins.

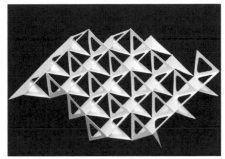

2 Card model of triangulated modules. Some of the faces are closed whilst others are left open, which, in addition to providing structural rigidity, enables greater variation of lighting effects.

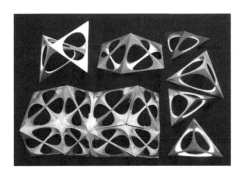

3 A subsequent card model illustrating a more uniform distribution of pattern and structure.

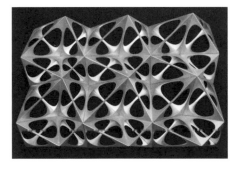

4 This informed a digital model of the spaceframe, which was further nuanced with apertures and rounding between the struts to offer stability.

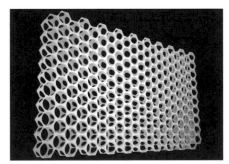

5 The digital model was then cast as a series of metal modules, using the data to generate formwork for the casting process.

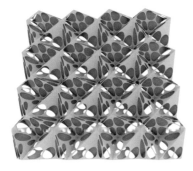

6 These modules were assembled to evaluate their properties in more detail.

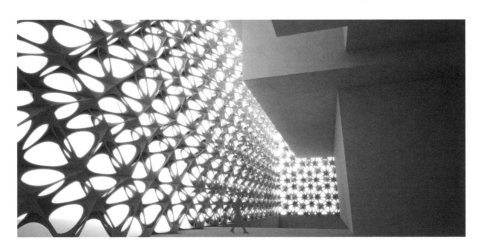

7 The resultant module was scaled and returned to the building context using a digital model.

Case study Forming doubly curved panels

Franken Architekten – Bubble, Frankfurt, 1999.

For their design at the BMW Trade Fair, Franken developed the concept of a drop of water to embody clean energy and sustainability. The Bubble was one of the first structures to be completely created with digital means, from design through to construction.

A, B, C AND D Digital simulation software was used to create the shape. In order for the building to appear as a giant water drop, the skin needed to express the balance between internal pressure and surface tension. Using film-animation software, the master geometry of the design was evolved parametrically.

E, F, G AND H The resultant design was then analyzed to explore structural and surface constraints, and areas of significant stress and loading.

I The building's frame was evolved from the parametric design model, and used to direct the fabrication of the 3,500 individual components that were jet-stream cut from sheet aluminium. These flat, orthogonal sections, when combined, form a three-dimensional double-curved form.

J The cladding elements, which comprised 305 unique acrylic-glass panels, were heat formed onto individually CNC-milled foam blocks.

K Once they had cooled, each panel was trimmed at the edges in preparation for connection to the substructure.

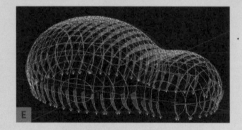
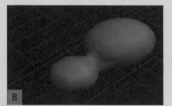
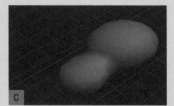
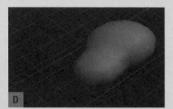

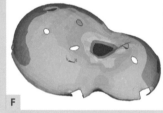
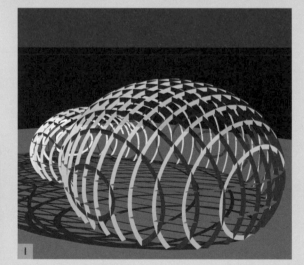
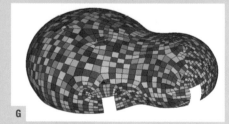
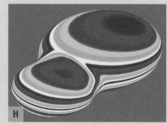
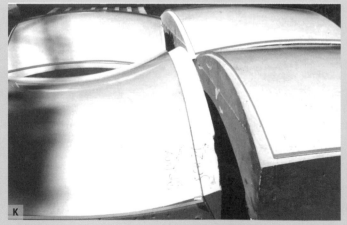

L AND M The Bubble remains a landmark project in the digital generation and manufacturing of buildings, showcasing the first example of a complete workflow of such techniques from start to finish.

Case study Forming components and continuous surfaces

3deluxe – CocoonClub, Frankfurt am Main, 2004; and Leonardo Glass Cube, Bad Driburg, 2007.

3deluxe is an interdisciplinary team from the fields of architecture; art; and interior, graphic, media and product design. From this broad spectrum of specialist knowledge, 3deluxe devises holistic design solutions that range from graphic identities via media installations to architecture – all displaying a coherent aesthetic. A key aspect of this work is the production of organic spaces, as exemplified by the two projects shown here.

The structure of the CocoonClub wall is reminiscent of a semi-permeable cell membrane. The two distinct layers of wall surface mounted in front of each other lends it additional depth. Air conditioning was installed between the layers so that the many 'pores' serve as ventilation openings.

A The membrane panels are formed using a casting process, and arrive on site as components.

B These are then stacked and attached to a steel frame, to give the appearance of a continuous semi-permeable skin.

C Detail view looking through the two layers.

The organically shaped, white DJ pulpit hosts all the media technology for the club, and is the central feature of the space. Its sculpted, curvilinear form was fabricated using forming to create sections that were then attached to a steel frame underneath.

D First sections are mounted to the substructure.

E Midway through the installation process.

F The completed form.

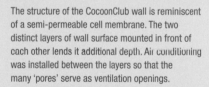

The Glass Cube structure comprises two formally contrasting elements: a geometrically stringent, cube-like shell volume and a free-form element positioned centrally in the interior. The undulating, curved white wall encases an introverted exhibition space, and its other side circumscribes the extroverted hallway along the glass façade. Three white sculptural structures – so-called 'Genetics' – connect the separate zones. On the glass façade, 'Genetics' appear again in a two-dimensional version. The construction of these sculptures necessitated a further, material-specific development. The major challenges were creating a joint-free surface and maintaining the dynamic form based on static principles – much easier to achieve using flexible textiles. The segmented shells of the 'Genetics' are compiled from deep-drawn half shells of a mineral material, which can be formed with heat as well as smoothed and ground. For their production, full-size models of the entire sculptures were made.

G The loadbearing structure comprises a steel support surrounded by a wood frame.

H Curved components are heat formed and delivered to site.

I These are connected together to ensure formal integrity prior to installation.

J The formed components are attached to the frame.

K Close-up view, illustrating various components around a 'Genetic' node.

L After assembly, the cross-joints were glued together, so that they were no longer visible.

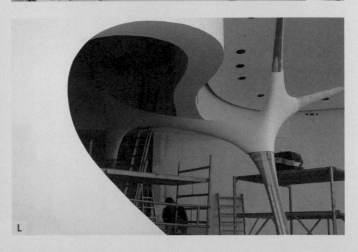

Case study Forming structural elements

Rogers Stirk Harbour + Partners – Berkeley Hotel Entrance Canopy, London, 1998–2005.

A Canopy design.

B Sketches for carbon-fibre beams.

C AND D Digital model for carbon-fibre beams.

E, F AND G Early prototype is assembled as a 1:1 section in the workshop.

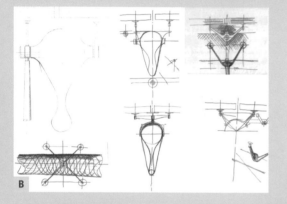

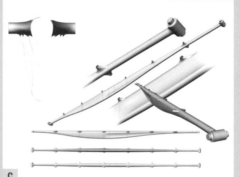

This new entrance to an existing building enabled exploration into the use of an innovative building material, carbon fibre. These structural elements were designed and modelled using Rhino, to easily shape the convex and concave surfaces in response to structural performance. The beams are thickest where the greatest torsion is, and more slender at the supports.

Carbon fibre is extremely lightweight, strong, fire resistant and can take any shape. The design included forms to accommodate stainless-steel fixings. Using a CNC milling fabrication technique, contractor Bellapart were able to make a positive mould of the main beam. From this, the 16 beams were moulded, the structure tested and made ready for installation.

H CNC-milled mould for forming beams.

I Prototype beams post-fabrication.

J Prototype support section.

K Detail of carbon-fibre beam showing typical surface pattern.

L Strength testing of beam.

7. Sectioning

Curvilinear geometry and methods of overlaying combine to form a complex structure in Zaha Hadid Architects' design for the Burnham Pavilion, Chicago. The pavilion comprises intricate bent-aluminum structural sections, each shaped and welded to create its unique curvilinear form. Outer and inner fabric skins wrap tightly around the metal frame to create the fluid shape. These skins also serve as the screen for video installations. The project aimed to maximize the recycling and reuse of materials after its role in Millennium Park. It can be installed for future use at another site.

Below
CAD drawings illustrating the complex geometry.

Sectioning is a method of profiling components in relation to a surface geometry. By taking a series of sectional cuts through a digital model, it offers a quick and effective way of gathering the necessary data to inform a CAD/CAM process. With the ongoing interest in and experimentation with complex, and often curvilinear, geometries, the ability to slice through the design to understand and communicate relationships of form, surface and space is highly beneficial. Digital modelling software commands typically provide instant sections through a three-dimensional form, and using a series of such sections in parallel it is immediately apparent how this will convert into a physical structure and surface. Whilst a relatively novel technique in the coupling of digital fabrication with architecture, it reflects a much longer tradition in shipbuilding and aeroplane construction. In these contexts, the form of the object is defined as a series of sections that are subsequently clad with a material or skin. Digital-fabrication techniques typically used in sectioning are cutters, particularly laser cutters and CNC routers, although, as with the process of folding, plasma and water-jet cutters expand the range of materials that may be worked in this manner. Sectioning was one of the primary tooling procedures that facilitated full-size prototyping, since the section profiles are essentially the same and may be scaled as required according to sheet material constraints.

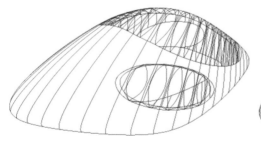

Left
The pavilion during the day, mirroring the design data of the digital model.

Below
The pavilion's transformation after dark, as lighting effects and projections radically alter its appearance.

Case study Sectioning a roof structure

Barkow Leibinger – Campus Restaurant and Event Space, Ditzingen, 2008.

A

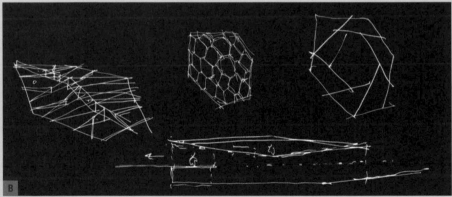

B

C

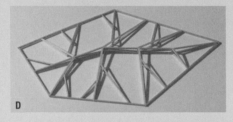

D

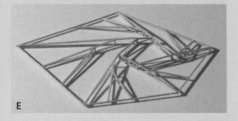

E

F

This pavilion provides a new central cafeteria and event space for Trumpf's campus and headquarters in Stuttgart. The canopy roof was developed as a polygonal leaf-like structure with long spans over groups of columns. This remarkable structure combines a steel frame and columns with glue-laminated wood-cell infill. The columns are intentionally located away from the beam perimeters and intersections to enhance the roof's cantilevered, hovering effect. While the steel allows large spans of up to 20m, the glulam infill was an attractive choice for its workability and sustainability. Hierarchically, the steel delineates a primary, vein-like structure while the glulam construction achieves a cellular web-like infill, completing the leaf analogy. The wood cells are functionally

'coded' and constructed as either skylights with solar-glass, perforated-wood acoustic planking (tying the roof diaphragm together); or as artificial lighting cells, modified by an aluminium honeycombed deflector. In order to economically achieve this highly complex structure, CNC routing and sawing was used to accommodate the more than 300 unique honeycomb joints. This is a particularly interesting development, as 'mass customization' is becoming essential, economically and time-wise, for an increasing number of the practice's projects.

A, B, C, D, E AND F Initial freehand sketches outline the original concept of a leaf-like, polygonal roof structure, and are made into physical models early in the design-development process to explore different types of structural arrangements and patterns.

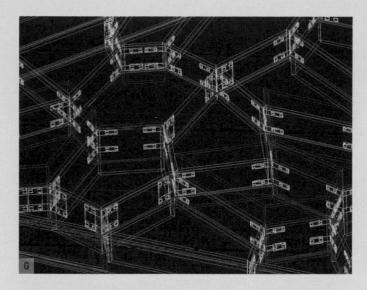

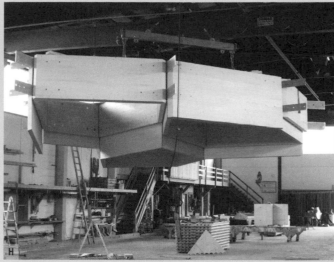

G The connections between each structural 'cell' are determined using three-dimensional digital-modelling software to ensure the integrity and performance both of elements and the composite whole.

H A full-size prototype of several structural cells allows the designers to inspect the aesthetic and structural characteristics of the roof.

I The finished project *in situ*, demonstrating its extensive spans on relatively minimal structure, and the skylights afforded by the innovative roof design.

Case study Sectioning as structural frame
Franken Architekten – Dynaform, Frankfurt am Main, 2001.

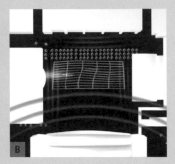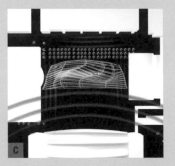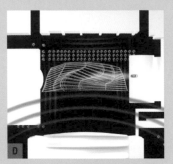

This exhibition pavilion for BMW aimed to express a dynamic sense of movement around the stationary cars inside. To achieve this the space was 'accelerated' using the Doppler effect, which was translated spatially along with the 'forces' of the surroundings to generate the parametric digital design for the building. This project uses a sectioning process to develop its design and fabrication data.

A, B, C AND D Form generation of the building, using forces derived from the immediate context.

E The bearing structure as a sequence of sections 'moving' through space to represent the fluidity of the design.

F AND G Sectioning is explicitly revealed during the process of assembly.

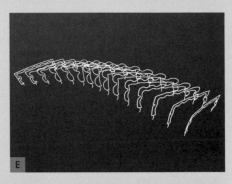

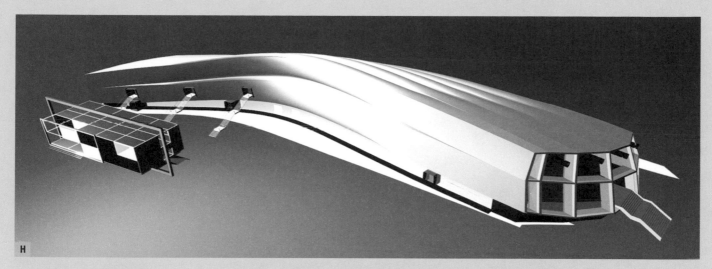

H Digital render, illustrating the dynamic design intention.

I AND J The completed building, echoing automotive geometry and notions of movement.

Case study Sectioning complex geometry
Rogers Stirk Harbour + Partners – Capodichino Metro Station, Naples, 2006–14.

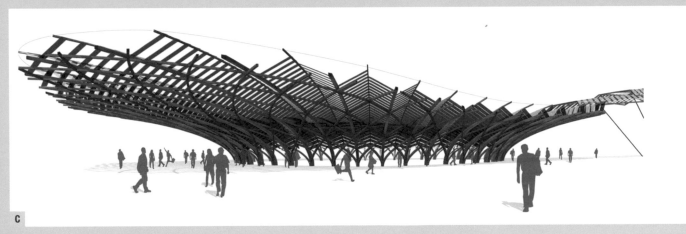

Parametric design provided the key generative and design-development tool for this metro-station roof. Its form was determined through a series of sunpath and movement studies, following the route that passengers take to and from departures and arrivals at Naples Capodichino Airport. By varying the sun and route parameters in a digital model, the architects were able to calculate the optimum roof form, and the density and angle of fixed louvres to give the greatest average shading to passengers on the most direct routes throughout the year. The design process initially resulted in each rib being a unique form. Once the form had been applied to elliptical sections of a toroid, the whole structure was greatly simplified to only 21 repeated elements. Thus, a self-supported structure was achieved through simple geometry that would have been inexpensive to build conventionally.

The roof is the central element of the station design, which utilizes complex geometry based on a toroid 3D shape with 46 main radial ribs. These ribs spring from the top of the station shaft, and each has a diameter of 33m across its inside faces. The maximum length of one rib is 39m and the area of the main canopy is 4,700m². The ribs are interconnected by diagonal struts, which stiffen the structure. These section sizes vary to suit their internal forces. The design has been parametrically optimized to minimize the number of elements needing to be fabricated. This, in turn, will simplify the construction process and, ultimately, ensure cost-effectiveness.

A AND B Digital renders of the proposed design.

C Digital model, showing roof in context.

D Early digital model, showing the roof as mapped from a toroid.

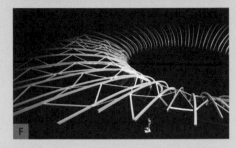

E AND F Physical model of the roof structure.

G Sectional model of the roof, illustrating the geometry.

H AND I Scale prototype of the roof structure, made for evaluative purposes.

Tiling as a geometric strategy is used extensively in the built environment, as shown by the tessellated pattern of this infrastructure element for the reshaping of the A2 ring road, Den Bosch (Netherlands), by UNStudio. The design's identity and coherence is expressed through the efficiency of the various elements, via a simple concept that lends itself to repetition. The concrete sound barriers are clad in a continuous relief, while the transparent barriers are printed with this same pattern – an abstracted migrating bird, which alludes to the identity of the A2 as a section of the trans-European Amsterdam–Palermo route.

8. Tiling

The process of tiling, also referred to as 'tessellating', involves the development of figures or shapes that when assembled together form a coherent plane without gaps or overlaps. Such tiles may have any geometric shape provided they fit together, even if the tiles change in size and shape across the plane itself. The patterned, tiled surfaces found in architecture are directly analogous to the mesh patterns defined using digital tiling tools. As with contouring, the history of tiling is long established in traditional manual craftsmanship – producing mosaics, stained-glass windows and other types of surface ornamentation. Time-consuming and labour-intensive, these precedents required the configuration of myriad fragments to form an intricate yet uniform design. Despite this, the cumulative result afforded considerable variation in terms of geometry, tone and overall image. One of the many advantages of digital design and fabrication methods is that they can effectively overcome the previous investment of time and also provide ways in which patterns may be generated and optimized to gain maximum impact both visually and materially – especially concerning the reduction of waste. During this book's first section, we discussed the use of meshes to approximate curvilinear geometry from polygons and triangulation. In the context of digital fabrication, the possibilities of translating design information from digital meshes to machines that produce components from sheet materials is immediately apparent. Therefore, this method of making complex three-dimensional forms and surfaces from a kit of essentially two-dimensional components has enabled architects to overcome one of greatest obstacles in fabricating this type of design. The development of mass customization and non-standard components, owing to the efficiency with which digital technologies may integrate these, has vastly expanded

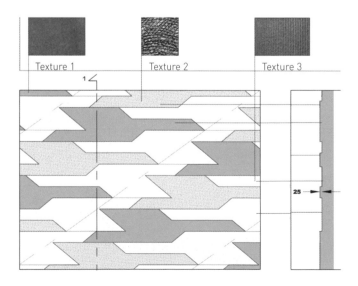

Left and middle
In Reiser + Umemoto's West Side Convergence project, the flowing design is structured using a triangulated tiling spaceframe that not only alludes to physical support and span but also reinforces the concept of uninterrupted, continuous information and material flux across the urban landscape of Manhattan.

Bottom
The canopy of the *Aurora* installation by Future Cities Lab features a tiling pattern to optimize the distribution of openings across its panels and maximize the variety of spatial effects through incorporated lighting elements.

3XN's design for Horten's new Copenhagen headquarters, completed in 2009, demonstrates innovative use of three-dimensional tessellation to address design issues. The façade elements were developed specifically for this building's complex geometry and based on a tiling pattern intended to facilitate a positive working environment, offering bay-window views towards the water while avoiding direct sunlight.

the field of design inquiry and options for modulation. As a result, designers can fabricate components with much more differentiation than hitherto, which, when combined, may produce effects in aesthetic, material and experiential terms that are much more transformative than the simple sum of their parts.

Tiled surfaces may either be smooth and precise, or faceted and primitive, factors that correspond to the degree of resolution. While it may appear preferable to always use a highly defined model, this can result in a very large file size, making it difficult to process and handle. Software platforms are increasingly adept at enabling designers to evaluate the resolution and size of the tiles in relation to the overall geometry, fabrication method and materials to be employed. This process of translation facilitates the design intentions to be calibrated with the proposed system of construction. Given the nature of tessellated patterns they are able to accommodate a wide range of tile and field designs, which has led to extensive application as a strategy for making complex form.

Case study Tiling as surface strategy
Barkow Leibinger – Trutec Building, Seoul, 2006.

This design uses digitally controlled 2D laser cutting to form 3D polygonal façade panels. The aluminium window extrusions, developed from a tiled surface geometry, transform a potentially ordinary office building by employing a custom-fabricated façade. Because the building's context was yet to be constructed, the façade was produced for optimal effect, forming a proactive 'camouflage' reflecting light, weather, people,

traffic, etc. in its proximity. Through the use of CNC cutting, standard off-the-shelf extrusions at angles were made, which were then connected to create shallow-depth 3D crystalline glazing panels. This process resulted in three basic types: a 2D panel, a 3D panel and a 3D panel rotated through 180 degrees. The combination of these types via a complex organizational matrix generated significant variation across the façade.

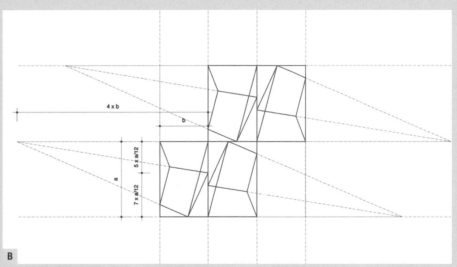

A Physical model of shallow-depth 3D panel.

B CAD drawing illustrating triangulated geometry, dimensions and tiling pattern formed through the transformation of rotation.

C, D, E, F, G AND H Study models produced at scale to evaluate lighting effects in relation to various tiling configurations.

I Weather testing, using a water turbine to assess the performance of several full-size prototype panels and the connections between them.

J Final panels being hoisted into place on site.

Case study Tiling to fabricate complex curvilinear form
Studio Gang – Marble Curtain, National Building Museum, Washington D.C., 2003.

An exploration of the structural capacity of stone, the Marble Curtain hung in tension from the museum's vaulted ceiling. Stone performs best when subjected to compressive loads. By linking pieces of stone together in a series of jigsaw-like chains, however, the Marble Curtain places the material in tension from the ceiling downwards, without any skeletal support or frame. No technical data exists for stone in tension; its capabilities were discovered by breaking stone types in a testing laboratory. Water-jet cutting allowed for intricate puzzle-shaped cuts. For structural redundancy, each piece was laminated with a fibre-resin backing. The Marble Curtain was 5.5m tall, comprised 620 pieces and weighed just 680kg. The stone was only 10mm thick, which allowed the design to explore its translucency.

A CAD drawing, indicating overall geometry of the design scaled within proposed context.

B Physical scale model, produced to evaluate the structural chains' positions.

C Testing of prototype 'jigsaw' pieces to understand performance of stone under tension.

D Jigsaw components are hung on the structural chains using a timber frame, which was subsequently removed once the curtain was fully hung.

A

B

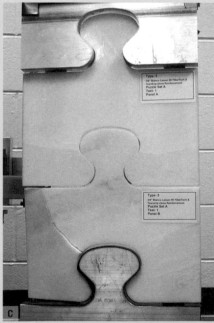

C

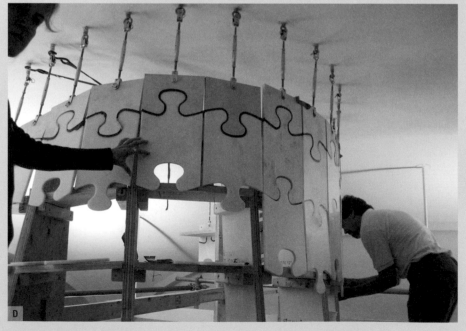

D

E The final installation, demonstrating the
resultant curved form and the translucence of
the stone owing to its minimal thickness.

STEP BY STEP TILING AND MASS CUSTOMIZATION

Surface deformations and curvilinear geometries are often mutually interdependent aspects of digital design. The fabrication techniques available to architects have enabled them to pursue explorative and innovative design inquiry and inform its realization. Faulders Studio's Deformscape project in San Francisco is a permanent outdoor living space at the rear of a private dwelling. Situated in a tightly packed neighbourhood, the single large Japanese Maple tree is used to establish a 'gravitational' pattern of grooves focused towards it.

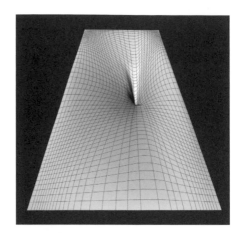

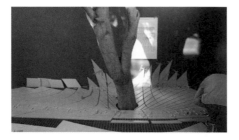

1 To generate the optically shifting pattern, a three-dimensional deformation is produced in 3D modelling software and then the wireframe grid is projected upward onto an implied 2D surface.

2 This is diagrammatically flattened to provide the pattern for CNC milling the individual marine-grade-plywood tiles, which are then painted.

3 The grid is also projected upward onto the rear wall, to create a geometric backdrop and further emphasize the optical illusion. The individual components are fixed to a porous fibre-reinforced polymer-grated surface to allow rainwater to drain laterally along the grooves to the tree's roots.

4 Once constructed, the flattened perspective regains its original, warped three-dimensionality. However, in reality the surface is entirely horizontal, enabling maximum use of the space.

STEP BY STEP TILING TO CREATE OPTIMAL VARIATION

Metal is an ideal material for folding since it retains shape, and complex and multiple folding is achievable via digital machines. This explorative project by Barkow Leibinger demonstrates the potential of metal tiles to create a three-dimensional surface, produced using a simple module that, once assembled with other identical counterparts, appears non-repetitive.

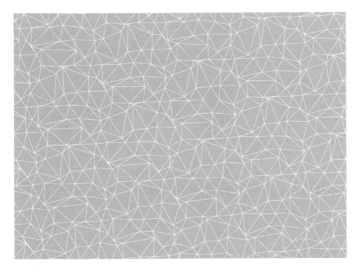

1 The tessellated pattern of the units' geometry is developed in CAD prior to application with material. The scripting technique enables mass-customized assembly from identical pieces to form a unique surface-making system.

2 The metal components are then two-dimensionally laser cut from flat stock and folded using the Trumabend machine.

3 Each component 'nests' into the next one in the surface composition, with 24 possible variations in which, when combined in a field as shown here, any repetition is concealed by the myriad permutations across the overall surface.

Case study Tiling as generative and fabrication processes

Future Cities Lab – *Xeromax Envelop{e}s*, various locations, 2010.

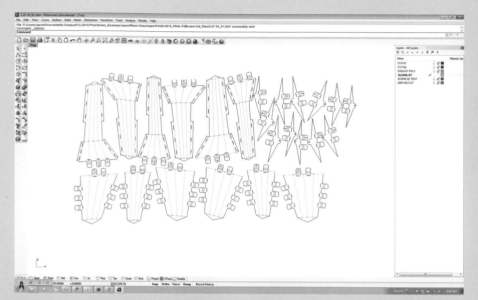

Future Cities Lab is an experimental design-and-research office based in San Francisco. Their work questions technology's role in contemporary society, exploring the intersections of design with advanced fabrication technologies, robotics, responsive building systems and public space. The *Xeromax Envelop{e}s* installation is an interactive and intricate geometric surface that pulsates in response to the movement of people close by.

For this project, digital design and fabrication allows the production of non-standard components and – although initially designed, fabricated and tested in San Francisco – the installation was then sent by standard post to New York, meaning it needed to be as light, modular and deployable as possible. The project was first modelled and fabricated using a combination of Grasshopper and Firefly (both plug-ins for Rhino). Its components were parametrically modelled and then individual pieces were flattened, tagged and organized on to digital-cut sheets that were laser cut. The primary construction materials were a synthetic waterproof paper and 2mm-thick clear and yellow sheets of polyester PET-G. The hexagonal surface comprises thousands of interconnected laser-cut pieces folded, notched, assembled and then hand sewn together using a fine stainless-steel cable. The robotic heads were constructed from both PET-G and cast-acrylic frames that held the electronics including LEDS, IR sensors and servomotors. All the electronics were custom fabricated by Future Cities Lab, and became an integral part of the installation's aesthetic. The final installation was suspended from the gallery ceiling using light-gauge aircraft cable.

A Digital-cutting pattern sheets, showing 'flat' geometry that when connected will form three-dimensional, hexagonal composites.

B Physical sketch models illustrate various ideas investigated during the design-development process. Different materials and geometrical configurations were produced, to interrogate their suitability for the overall system.

C Assembly of the modules, from two-dimensional cut pieces to three-dimensional faceted objects.

D Testing the circuits and programming of servomotors.

E Electronic circuitry is combined with the installation's plastic infrastructure.

F Connecting the laser-cut panels to form the responsive surface membrane.

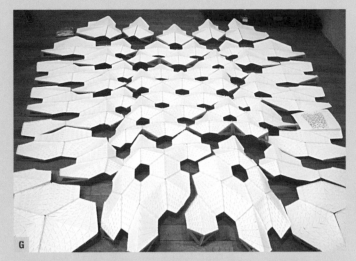

G The layout of modules prior to integration into a continuous surface.

H Connecting the surface modules together.

I Suspending the installation within the gallery space.

J View from behind the surface.

K Final installation: surface becomes further articulated as it responds to the movement of people within its domain.

Future fabrication of architecture

The impact of digital design and fabrication techniques on architecture is already far-reaching. The integration of digitally generated data to produce precise and complex geometry, to direct making and assembly processes, and exploit material performance is returning architects to a position that had disappeared with the masterbuilders of medieval times. The future of digital fabrication in architecture therefore implies rich and varied dialogue of exploration, invention and application. The seminal Fabrication conference held at the University of Waterloo in Cambridge, Ontario in 2004 may be recognized as a major impetus in this movement, which has been further substantiated by various events, projects and exhibitions – perhaps most significantly the FABRICATE: Making Digital Architecture conference held at The Bartlett School of Architecture in London in 2011. The latter provided a global summit and update from many of the leading figures, practices and organizations immersed in this joint quest for creativity, proving just how far and wide the developments have been in such a short period of time. The multiplicity of contemporary approaches in digital fabrication is considerable, but the recurrent theme of how we collaborate and best apply our design intelligence remains essential to these endeavours.

Perhaps the most immediate transformation for digital fabrication is connected to the widespread availability and mobility of the equipment and techniques. It is now possible for designers to own, and even self-assemble, 3D printers and for design offices and architectural practices to accommodate these along with CNC manufacturing processes as an extended part of their studio. Such facilities were prohibitively expensive only a decade ago. This development, coupled with increasingly user-friendly graphic interfaces on software platforms, is allowing a broader community of designers to experiment with fabrication processes. Architecture schools have generally been quick to adopt CAD/CAM resources and students and researchers continue to push the limits of existing technologies in pursuit of knowledge and further development. Moreover, digital fabrication methods have already had, and will continue to have, major implications for the design, production and delivery of buildings. This will become particularly relevant if such techniques are to be used to generate and build designs on a large scale. Therefore, the intelligence within these systems and how it may be developed, whether embodied artificially or physically – such as to inform assembly and building protocols, or to enable performative functionality and dynamic behaviour – are also paramount. This issue is especially important given the direct relationship, and feedback potential, between design and construction data that is intrinsic to digital fabrication approaches.

A further area of investigation is the behaviour of materials and their potential to be computational tools in themselves, enabling responsiveness. Experimentation with the molecular structure of materials and their performance characteristics under different conditions is already a feature of some research projects included in this publication but therein lie more unchartered territories and untapped knowledge. Integrating material behaviour with detailed geometrical data may facilitate a level of material computation that will transform construction processes and allow responsive properties at the scale of material substructure and organization to be factored into design intent.

The architectural projects currently underway reinforce these various trajectories and suggest the ways in which this ever-mutating and increasingly influential area of development may continue to cross-pollinate with other disciplines, flourish and inspire. The more designers who embrace these opportunities, the greater the degree of knowledge transfer and application of digital fabrication that will arise.

The breakthroughs in ubiquitous computing may be enriched by the increasing accessibility and affordability of digital fabrication equipment. Products such as the Thing-O-Matic® by Makerbot Industries enable designers to assemble a 3D printer kit for personal manufacturing.

Case study Responsive architectural surfaces

μ:) Microhappy/Marilena Skavara – Adaptive Fa[CA]de, 2009.

Adaptive Fa[CA]de is an emergent, adaptive building skin that aims to provide optimum light levels to an interior. The project was developed as part of Marilena Skavara's MSc thesis in Adaptive Architecture and Computation at the Bartlett. Using the computational and behavioural characteristics of Cellular Automata (CA) coupled with artificial intelligence, it gradually 'learns' from its own errors to inform future behaviour.

A, B, C AND D 3D printing facilitated fabrication of the tile supports, which were then connected on pivot joints and wired up to servo motors.

E, F, G, H, I AND J The various patterns performed by the façade in response to surrounding light levels help the design behave as a 'living skin'. Developed to provide optimal light intensity to the interior, the kinetic interplay, as light source and levels change, posits an engaging area of potential application for performative architecture.

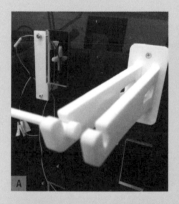

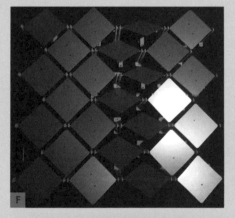
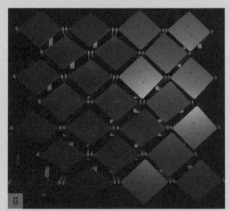

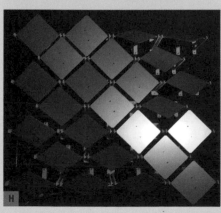

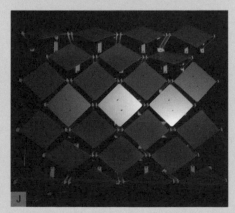

Case study Digital fabrication on the move
Gramazio & Kohler – Pike Loop, Manhattan, New York, 2009.

The synergy between the research and practice of Gramazio & Kohler has enabled the development of innovative fabrication processes and their implementation in architectural design. Pike Loop is a 22m-long structure made of brick, the most traditional building material in New York, and was designed for installation on site by an industrial robot from a movable truck trailer. Over 7,000 bricks aggregate to form an infinite loop that weaves along the pedestrian island. The continuous form and homogeneous expression of the structure can only be achieved through on-site digital fabrication. The structure is built using the robotic fabrication unit R-O-B housed in a transportable freight container. R-O-B was shipped from Switzerland to New York and loaded onto a low-bed trailer for transport and on-site fabrication. Moving the truck trailer shifts the 4.5m work area of R-O-B along the site in order to build the complete structure.

A Positioned *in situ*, the robotic fabrication unit carries out a programmed test to check its operability.

B More than 7,000 bricks form an 'infinite' loop along the pedestrian island.

C As each brick is laid within the choreographed composition, the 'woven' wall's form emerges.

D The precision of the robotic operations is illustrated here as the complex geometry of the design is replicated on site.

E In changing rhythms, the loop lifts off the ground and intersects with itself at peaks and valleys.

F The digitally designed brick structure is further articulated using a weighted compressing and tensioning of the brick bond. Where the loop 'flies', the bond becomes stretched and thus lighter; where it brings loads to the ground it becomes jagged and heavier, thus wider and more stable.

G The completed installation.

Case study Embedded intelligence in self-assembly systems

Skylar Tibbits – Logic Matter, Massachusetts Institute of Technology, 2010.

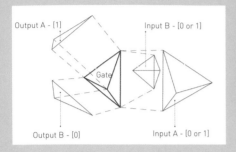

Left

Right-angle tetrahedron demonstrating the functionality of a NAND gate through input, output and gate decisions. Output A and Output B are the two output faces, either [0] or [1]. Input A and Input B are the two input faces. The input faces can both receive either [0] or [1] at any time. The input faces will dictate the decision in the Gate unit as to which face (Output A [1] or Output B [0]) will be utilized, directly based on the NAND truth table.

Below

The self-assembly system enables considerable variation in the programmable sequences of growth. Binary gradient sequences and resultant spatial output. Orange units are inputs equal to 1 whilst grey units are gates.

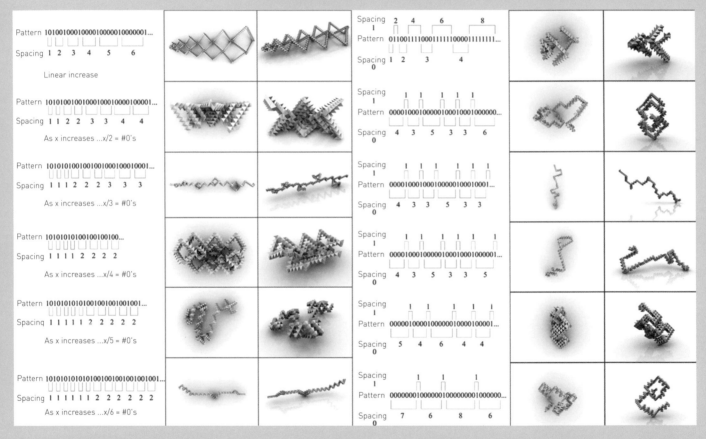

The research of Skylar Tibbits addresses the contrast between current modes of assembly and the output of digital design tools to develop responses to the increasing complexity of the built environment. The central theme of his work is self-assembly in relation to the future of manufacturing, production and construction. The Logic Matter project is a system of passive mechanical digital logic modules for self-guided assembly of large-scale structures. In contrast to existing systems in self-reconfigurable robotics, Logic Matter introduces scalability, robustness, redundancy and local heuristics to achieve passive assembly. This is developed as a mechanical module that implements digital NAND logic as an effective tool for encoding local and global assembly sequences. Logic Matter seeks to facilitate material computing and material-provided commands for the user whilst utilizing the power of digital information for precise in construction.

Above
4 Logic Matter modules demonstrating
programmability of base configuration.

Left
60 unit working prototype demonstrating 3D single-
path and user programmability. Grey units behave
as NAND gates while white units are inputs.

Case study Computational materiality as integrative approach

Phil Ayres – The Persistent Model, CITA, Royal Danish Academy of Fine Arts, 2009–12.

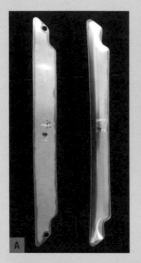

A AND B Free-form metal inflation is a fabrication process that derives from hydroforming except no die is used to inform the sheet material. Instead, two sheets of metal are welded together to form a sealed cushion into which a fluid medium is introduced. This material organization inflates as the internal pressure increases, pushing the material beyond its elastic limit and into the phase of plastic deformation.

C Progressive Material Transform: the initial digital representation informs the cutting of the steel profiles that make up the cushions. This representation becomes redundant after inflation, requiring re-informing.

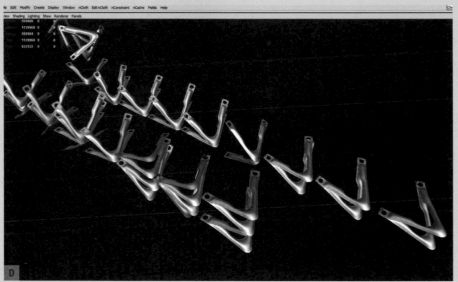

This research project led by Phil Ayres at the Centre for Information Technology and Architecture (CITA), investigates a design strategy that couples representation and artefact in a circular relationship as a means of managing indeterminacy throughout the various phases of architectural activity, namely: design, fabrication/construction and occupancy/use. This proposition maintains the instrumental capacity of representation as a space of speculation and specification, while addressing issues pertaining to the ideal, predictive and pre-determined characteristics of representational methods in relation to contexts of use that tend towards the endemically dynamic and contingent.

The Persistent Model considers the site of indeterminacy as the fabric of the construct itself. Free-form metal inflation provides a conceptually congruent material veil to these concerns. It is a procedure through which outcomes deviate from initializing representations with greater or lesser degrees of predictability – a result of a sensitive dependency established between material behaviour and the nature of the imposed geometry. This deviation requires feedback mechanisms for the artefact to re-inform the representation.

D Compound Movements: investigating jointing positions digitally to drive spatial development. Components are aggregated in such a manner that local transformations impact the overall compound.

E This early experiment with the hydroforming process to inflate metal took the structure to failure point so that material responses could be analyzed and incorporated into later stages of the project. As the inflation process continues, dramatic transformations occur to the components' formal and performance properties resulting largely from permanent buckling.

As components are inflated they dramatically transform in formal and performance characteristics – these transformations are an outcome of material behaviour steered through imposed geometry. The simplicity of the forming process belies a complex matrix of interactions occurring within and between a variety of microstructures (atomic lattice and grains) and macrostructures (component and aggregate). The resultant coupling of digital and material creates a dialogue between iteration and transformation, which is simultaneously construct and process. The potential to gain further insight of material behaviours through such novel fabrication processes may subsequently inform how to best represent and guide these and establish their design criteria for greater application in architecture.

F Nested Feedback System: the environment of representation is nested within the environment of operation so that the ideal feeds into the actual, the actual feeds back to the ideal and a tempered ideal feeds back to the actual. Control is passed and shared through the feedback loop created.

G Constraint Context: sequential inflation constructs a sensitive site dependency which is monitored and creates a cybernetic loop as both parts of the system, digital and material, feedback to each other.

Conclusion

Below
The Decibot is part of the larger *bot family of programmable folding chains by Skylar Tibbits. The *bot family contains electromechanical folding at varying lengths. This is the largest of the family with overall dimensions of 365 x 45 x 45cm unfolded and 91 x 91 x 91cm folded into a cube.

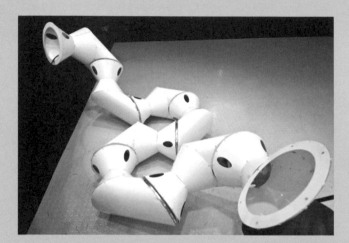

Digital fabrication signals a major shift in the way we may engage architectural design. The techniques used by digital fabrication require designers to rethink their design process, often developing novel methodologies and non-linear approaches. By allowing the generation, integration and strategies of creative ideas and manufacturing operations to inform each other in a meaningful way, the potential of digital fabrication may be fully realized. Key to this development is an interest in and exploration of materials and how design intent may be connected or expressed through their employment. The creative use of computation to develop digital tools has been integral to many of the projects featured in this book. Given that such tools provide the interface between design and fabrication, the experimentation and customization afforded by them should offer a wealth of opportunities for those willing to immerse themselves in their development. Indeed, the forays envisaged for one tool may lead to other applications resulting in further knowledge transfer and exploration. Therefore, tools should deepen our inquisitive nature rather than simply become reductive and convenient.

The opportunities afforded by digital fabrication have had a two-fold impact. Firstly, a new generation of innovative, motivated, highly skilled programmers and designers are engaging in a discourse with materials and fabrication processes with groundbreaking results. Secondly, the integration of digital design and fabrication technologies to deliver building components and systems through robust and streamlined digital workflows is growing steadily as the benefits of simultaneous and feedback mechanisms become more apparent. Perhaps most exciting of all, architectural designers are increasingly working in an interdisciplinary manner that, far from diluting their field, has led to advanced expertise, bringing them back into the processes of manufacture and construction, from which they had become distant. These shifts in the design and making of architecture are characterized by an abundant generosity in knowledge sharing and collaborative production. The growing influence of these technologies within architecture is evident in numerous exhibitions and an ever-expanding body of literature on the subject, as well as the gradual increase in digitally fabricated buildings and interventions in our cities, public spaces and landscapes.

Below left and right
Neri Oxman's interdisciplinary research is deeply embedded in the production possibilities of techniques and material limits. Her Subterrain project explores the notion of material organization in relation to the distribution and magnitude of forces shaping a physical terrain. Analysis of material behaviour in relation to properties and performance allows the interaction between directional morphology and direction of various stresses to be modelled. This data is subsequently reconstructed using a CNC milling process and a variety of timbers to produce laminated structural composites that may inform larger uses in buildings.

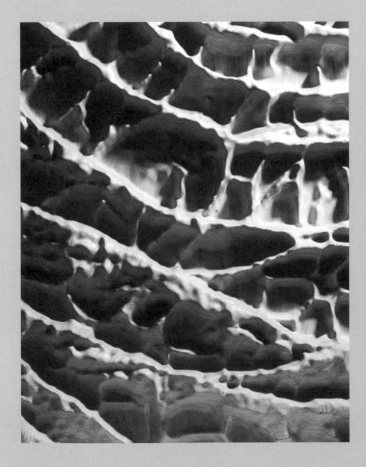

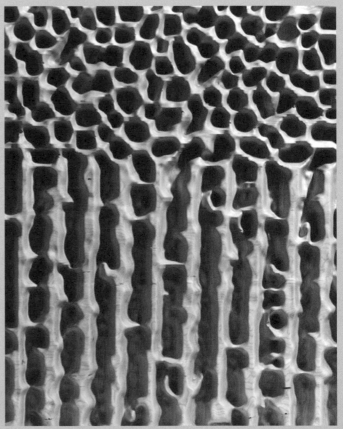

Glossary

algorithm

In the context of digital design, an algorithm is a series of clearly defined instructions that enable a computational procedure to be carried out. Algorithms are intrinsic to digital design software with different platforms enabling varying degrees of potential interaction with the computer script itself.

Boolean logic

This type of algebra underpins computational programmes, machine code and assembly languages and differs from the more commonly used elementary algebra since it specifically deals with the values 0 and 1. These may be thought of as two integers, or as the 'truth' values *false* and *true* respectively. In either case they are referred to as binary digits or bits, in contrast to the decimal digits 0 through to 9.

Computer-Aided Design (CAD)

The use of a software program as a tool to design an object. A CAD file is required to control a CAM machine.

Computer-Aided Manufacture (CAM)

The use of computer software to control a machine tool or process. A CAM machine requires a CAD file to work from.

Computer-Aided Three-dimensional Interactive Application (CATIA) modelling

CATIA enables surfacing, reverse engineering, and visualization solutions to create, modify, and validate complex innovative shapes. The software allows the designer to fabricate 3D components, using 3D sketches, from sheet metal, composites, moulded, forged or tooling parts up to the definition of mechanical assemblies.

Computational Fluid Dynamic (CFD)

This is a branch of fluid mechanics that uses numerical methods and algorithms to solve and analyze problems that involve fluid flows. The development of advanced software platforms has enabled this information to be visualized and the effects predicted in a very precise manner.

Computer Numerical Control (CNC) milling and routing

CNC milling and routing machines can cut three-dimensional objects or surfaces, using a CAD file, from a solid material such as timber, aluminium, polystyrene foams and carbon fibres. The machines can cut along three or more axes simultaneously, enabling 3D forms to be created.

Finite Element Analysis (FEA)

This is a software platform that facilitates detailed visualization of where structures bend or twist, and indicates the distribution of stresses and displacements. Such software may also enable specific properties to be examined including thermal, fluid, and dynamic structural environments. In the context of digital fabrication, FEA can be very valuable in producing stiffness and strength visualizations and therefore also in minimizing weight, materials and costs.

laser cutting

A laser cutter can slice through a material or engrave a pattern on to its surface using a CAD file. The technique can be used to sculpt a range of materials, including plastics, textiles, wood, board and paper.

meshes

These provide a method for generating complex geometry and are typically polygonal or polyhedral. In either type, the mesh approximates a geometric domain through an arrangement of 'vertices', 'edges' and 'faces' that combine to define the shape of the desired object.

morphogenesis

The evolutionary development of form in an organism, or part thereof, is known as morphogenesis. By understanding that living organisms may be viewed as systems – and that these evolve their often complex forms and behavioural patterns as a result of interactions between their components over time –dynamic, biological growths and transformations may also be simulated within digital design processes.

Non-Uniform Rational Basis Spline (NURBS)

NURBS is a mathematical model typically used in digital design for generating and representing curves and surfaces. This type of curve provides both considerable flexibility and precision for handling both analytic and freeform shapes and provides an effective design tool for integrating complex geometry within architectural design.

parametric design

Parametric design enables the designer to define relationships between elements or groups of elements, and to assign values or expressions to organize and control those definitions. It addresses the constraints of traditional CAD operations as – instead of the designer interacting directly with individual design elements – it creates a series of relationships allowing elements to connect and build up the design. The designer may, at any time, alter the values or equations that form the relationships between elements and the effects of these changes will be incorporated across the entire system.

plasma-arc cutting

This is a process typically used to cut steel and other metals. An inert gas is passed through a nozzle at high speed and in conjunction with an electrical arc, which turns some of the gas into plasma that is at such a high temperature it can cut through the metal.

rapid prototyping

Rapid prototyping machines 'print' in three dimensions from a CAD file. The object is built up layer-by-layer; each new layer is bonded or melted into the previous one. Rapid prototyping can be undertaken in a variety of different materials, for example: polyamide powder or nylon, plaster bonded with glue, photo-polymer resin, bronze alloy, steel, stainless steel or cobalt chrome. Types of rapid prototyping include:

• **Direct Metal Laser Sintering (DMLS)**, which prints three-dimensionally using a variety of metals, including bronze alloy, steel, stainless steel and cobalt chrome.

• **Fused Deposition Modelling (FDM)**, which forms layers by extruding small beads of thermoplastic material that hardens immediately after extrusion.

• **Selective Laser Sintering (SLS)**, which builds three-dimensionally using a polyamide powder.

- **stereolithography**, which uses a vat of liquid UV-curable photopolymer and a UV laser to form layers of cross-section on the surface of the liquid which are incrementally cured through exposure to the laser's light.

- **3D printing**, which prints three-dimensionally using a plaster-based material bonded with glue.

3D scanning
A 3D scanner digitally records the three-dimensional properties of an object to create a CAD file. The digital object can then be manipulated or recreated. A digitizing arm is a type of 3D scanner.

voxel
A voxel, also known as a volumetric pixel or Volumetric Picture Element, is a volume element that represents a value on a regular grid in 3D space.

water-jet cutting
A water-jet cutter uses a fine jet of water, mixed with abrasive matter, to cut a range of hard materials, including iron, steel, titanium, stone, concrete, glass, laminated wood, mirrors and composite resins.

Further reading

Aldersey-Williams, H. & Antonelli, P. [eds] (2008) *Design and the Elastic Mind.* The Musuem of Modern Art (New York).

Aranda, B. & Lasch, C. (2006) *Tooling.* Pamphlet Architecture no. 27. Princeton Architectural Press.

Ayres, P. [ed.] (2012) *Persistent Modelling: Extending the Role of Architectural Representation.* Routledge.

Barkow, F. & Leibinger, R. (2009) *An Atlas of Fabrication.* Architectural Association.

Burry, M. (2011) *Scripting Cultures: Architectural design and programming.* John Wiley & Sons.

Callicott, N. (2001) *Computer-Aided Manufacture in Architecture: The Pursuit of Novelty.* Architectural Press.

Chaszar, A. [ed.] (2006) *Blurring the Lines.* Wiley-Academy.

Coates, P. (2010) *Programming.Architecture.* Routledge.

Colletti, M. [ed.] (2010) *Exuberance.* John Wiley & Sons.

Corser, R. [ed.] (2010) *Fabricating Architecture: Selected Readings in Digital Design and Manufacturing.* Princeton Architectural Press.

Cruz, M. & Pike, S. [eds] (2008) *Neoplasmatic Design.* John Wiley & Sons.

Dunn, N. (2010) *Architectural Modelmaking.* Laurence King.

Frazer, J. (1995) *An Evolutionary Architecture.* Architectural Association.

Freyer, C., Noel, S. & Rucki, E. (2008) *Digital by Design: crafting technology for products and environments.* Thames & Hudson.

Glynn, R. & Sheil, B. [eds] (2011) *FABRICATE: Making Digital Architecture.* Riverside Architectural Press.

Gramazio, F. & Kohler, M. (2008) *Digital Materiality in Architecture.* Lars Müller Publishers.

Hensel, M., Menges, A. & Weinstock, M. (2004) *Emergence: Morphogenetic Design Strategies.* John Wiley & Sons.

Hensel, M. & Menges, A. (2006) *Morpho-Ecologies.* AA Publications.

Hoverstadt, L. (2009) *Beyond the Grid: Architecture and Information Technology.* Birkhäuser.

Iwamoto, L. (2009) *Digital Fabrications: Architectural and Material Techniques.* Princeton Architectural Press.

Kieran, S. & Timberlake, J. (2004) *Refabricating Architecture.* McGraw-Hill.

Kolarevic, B. [ed.] (2003) *Architecture in the Digital Age: Design and Manufacturing.* Spon Press.

Kolarevic, B. & Klinger, K. [eds] (2008) *Manufacturing Material Effects: Rethinking Design and Making in Architecture.* Routledge.

Lally, S. & Young, J. [eds] (2007) *Softspace: From a Representation of Form to a Simulation of Space.* Routledge.

Leach, N., Turnbull, D. & Williams, C. [eds.] (2004) *Digital Tectonics.* Wiley-Academy.

Littlewood, D. [ed.] (2008) *Space Craft: Developments in Architectural Computing.* RIBA Publishing.

Lynn, G. (1999) *Animate Form.* Princeton Architectural Press.

Meredith, M. & Sasaki, M. [eds] (2008) *From Control to Design: Parametric/Algorithmic Architecture.* Actar.

Oxman, R. & Oxman, R. [eds] (2010) *The New Structuralism.* John Wiley & Sons.

Picon, A. (2010) *Digital Culture in Architecture: An Introduction for the Design Professions.* Birkhäuser.

Pottmann, H., Asperl, A., Hofer, M. & Kilian, A. (2007) *Architectural Geometry.* Bentley Institute Press.

Reiser, J. & Umemoto, N. (2006) *Atlas of Novel Tectonics.* Princeton Architectural Press.

Schröpfer, T. (2011) *Material Design: Informing Architecture by Materiality.* Birkhäuser.

Sheil, B. [ed.] (2008) *Proto Architecture: Analogue and Digital Hybrids.* John Wiley & Sons.

Sheil, B. (2012) *Manufacturing the Bespoke: Making and Prototyping Architecture.* John Wiley & Sons.

Spuybroek, L. (2004) *NOX: Machining Architecture.* Thames & Hudson.

Terzidis, K. (2003) *Expressive Form: A Conceptual Approach to Computational Design.* Spon Press.

Terzidis, K. (2006) *Algorithmic Architecture.* Architectural Press.

Thomas, K. L. (2007) *Material Matters: Architecture and Material Practice.* Routledge.

Woodbury, R. (2010) *Elements of Parametric Design.* Routledge.

Index

Dini, Enrico 107
Direct Metal Laser Sintering 186

E
Eames, Charles and Ray 16
Ecotect software *33*
emergence 18, *57*, 66, 68, 78, 120, 177
EMERGENT/Tom Wiscombe
  Batwing *21*, 78–9
  Dragonfly, SCI-Arc, Los Angeles *55*, 58–9
  Garak Fish Market, Seoul *11*
  Lizard Panel prototype *79*
  MoMA/P.S.1 Urban Beach, Queens, New York *33*, 146–7
  Performing Arts Centre, Taipei *37*
  Thermo-strut prototype *79*
  Tracery Glass prototype *79*

F
Fab Lab programme, Center for Bits and Atoms, MIT 26
FABRICATE: Making Digital Architecture conference, Bartlett School of Architecture, London (2011) 176
Fabrication conference, University of Waterloo, Cambridge, Ontario (2004) 176
façades
  and algorithms *62*
  in case studies 72–3, 114–15, 128–9, 144–5, 169
  non-standard *84*
  patterns *11, 12, 50,* 72–3, 114, *115, 151, 177*
  responsive *22, 42, 48,* 128–9, 144–5, 169
  tiling *168,* 169
Faulders Studio/Thom Faulders
  Airspace, Tokyo *11,* 72–3
  BAMscape, Berkeley Art Museum, California 131
  Deformscape project, San Francisco 172
  GEOtube, Dubai *122*
feedback 16, *58, 78,* 112, *125,* 176, 182, *183,* 185
FHNW, Switzerland 123
'file-to-factory' process 77, *98*
Finite Element Analysis (FEA) 44
Firefly (Rhino plug-in) 174
Flatwriter (Friedman) 16–17
folding *10, 78, 93,* 140–7, 173, *184*
  case studies 64–5, 142, 144–7
Foreign Office Architects (FOA)
  International Airport, Shenzhen *36*
  New Street Station, Birmingham *22*
  Yokohama International Port Terminal *10*
formative processes *57,* 89, *96, 122 see also* forming
forming 148–57

case studies 152–7
step by step techniques 150–1
Franken Architekten
  Bubble, BMW Trade Fair, Frankfurt, Germany 152–3
  Dynaform pavilion for BMW, Frankfurt, Germany 162–3
  'Liquid Wall,' Home Couture project, Berlin *49*
  Take Off, Terminal 2, Munich Airport *52*
Frazer, John 16, *17,* 18
Friedman, Yona 16–17
Fused Deposition Modelling (FDM) 102, 104, *106*
Future Cities Lab
  Aurora installation *21, 45, 167*
  Glaciarium installation, New York 80–1
  Vivisys installation *54*
  Xeromax Envelop{e}s installation 174–5

G
G-code instructions (CNC milling and routing) 96, 99
Gaudí, Antoni 68
Gehry & Associates: Disney Concert Hall, Los Angeles *20,* 22
generative design and software 18, 27, 55, 60, 69, *114,* 124 *see also* parametric design
GenerativeComponents software 27, *54*
Generator Interface (Frazer and Price) *17*
Giacometti, Bruno *53*
Google SketchUp software 27
Gorbet, Rob 46
Goulthorpe, Mark *see* dECOi
Gramazio & Kohler
  Designers' Saturday project, Langenthal, Switzerland 123
  Gantenbein Vineyard, Fläsch, Switzerland 114–15
  mTable 132–3
  Pike Loop, Manhattan, New York 178–9
  Structural Oscillations, Swiss Pavilion, Venice 53
  West Fest Pavilion, Wettswil am Albis, Switzerland *76*
Grasshopper (Rhino plug-in) 27, 174
Greg Lynn FORM
  Fountain of Toys, Los Angeles *77*
  light feature *148*
  Swarovski Crystal Palace *9*
Griffiths, Rupert *99*
  Manchester street furniture *92*

H
Hadid, Zaha
  Burnham Pavilion, Millennium Park, Chicago *158, 159*
  Heydar Aliyev Cultural Centre, Baku *21, 35*
  Mobile Art Pavilion for Chanel *7*

Nordpark Cable Railway, Innsbruck *50*
One North Masterplan, Singapore 56–7
Hansmeyer, Michael: Subdivided Column project *76,* 85
Hasenkopf *77*
hybrid techniques *10,* 77–83
  case studies 78–83

I
IBM System/360 computer 16
indeterminacy 24, 60, 120, 182
interactivity *13, 18, 19, 54, 61,* 86
Iwamoto, Lisa 20

J
jigs *77,* 80

K
Kelley, Thomas (Future Cities Lab) 80–1
kinetics *49, 52, 143, 177*
Kokkugia: Fibrous Tower project *7*
Kokkugia: Babiy Yar – Inverted Monument project *62*
Kolarevic, Branko 23, 42, 68, 120

L
Labbe, Fred (Expedition Engineering) *60*
Laminated Object Manufacturing (LOM) 102
laser cutters *27,* 90
laser cutting 88, 90–5, 186
  advantages 90, 91
  case study 94–5
  and folding 140–1, *142*
  limitations 90, 91
  patterns *9,* 64, 90, 91, *142,* 186
  and sectioning 158
  and tiling 169
laser sintering 186 *see also* Selective Laser Sintering
layout sheets 97, *98,* 101
Lénárd, Ilona *see* ONL
Lloyd Jones, Peter 25

M
macdowell tomova: wavePavilion, Taubman College of Architecture, Michigan 112
Marjot, Timothieus
  mass customized housing project *84*
  Natural Code pavilion project 124
mass customization 77, 84, *133,* 160, 166, 172, *173*
material technology and research *12,* 113
  case study 182–3
  and digital fabrication *9, 23,* 70, 76, *77,* 156, 176, 184, *185*
  and morphogenesis *67,* 70–1
Matter Design

Acknowledgements

This book is essentially parametric in nature. As a system of relational elements, which are all remarkable for their quality and integrity, it has become much greater than the sum of its parts. With this in mind, I wish to first and foremost express my considerable gratitude to all the individuals, practices and organizations that generously contributed their material. In particular I would like to thank: Patrick Drewello, who provided significant zeal, material and feedback; the students of [Re_Map] and Daniel Richards for continuing to advance the field of digital architecture through innovative enquiry; Jim Backhouse and Sue Merrill for their dedication to the cause; my colleagues at the Manchester School of Architecture for engaging discussions and encouragement along the way; John Hyatt and the Manchester Institute for Research & Innovation in Art & Design (MIRIAD) for supporting the research that went into this book; Philip Cooper and Sophie Wise of Laurence King for their advice and patience during the production of this publication; and my family and friends whose support and understanding enabled it to be written. Finally, I would like to acknowledge the openness, energy and commitment of the digital fabrication community, whose evolution and innovation never ceases to surprise, delight and inspire – long may this collective design intelligence continue.

Picture credits

T top, L left, R right, M middle, B bottom

1 Future Cities Lab: **3** Skylar Tibbits; **5** Barkow Leibinger; **6L** NOX; **6R** Supermanoeuvre; **7TL** Kokkugia; **7R** Zaha Hadid Architects / John Linden; **7B** Coop Himmelb(l)au; **8 all** Amanda Levete Architects / Gidon Fuehrer; **9T** Greg Lynn FORM; **9BL** Reiser + Umemoto; **9BR** Barkow Leibinger; **10T** Office for Metropolitan Architecture; **10M** MVRDV; **10B** Foreign Office Architects / Satoru Mishima; **11T** Tom Wiscombe/EMERGENT; **11B** Faulders Studio / Studio M; **12T** Coop Himmelb(l)au; **12BL** UNStudio / Christian Richters; **12BR** Wiel Arets Architects; **13T** ONL (Oosterhuis_Lénárd); **13B** Neri Oxman; **14** Courtesy of the Computer History Museum; **15T** Courtesy of the Computer History Museum; **15B** Dennis Crompton © Archigram 1964; **16T** Gordon Pask; **16B** Courtesy of the Computer History Museum; **17** John and Julia Frazer; **18** John Frazer / Architectural Association; **19T** Diller Scofidio + Renfro; **19M** Coop Himmelb(l)au; **19B** Skylar Tibbits; **20** Nick Dunn; **21 T** Zaha Hadid Architects; **21 M** Future Cities Lab (Johnson and Gattegno); **21B** Tom Wiscombe / EMERGENT; **22** Foreign Office Architects; **23L** Gramazio & Kohler, Architecture and Digital Fabrication, ETH Zurich; **23R** Mark Goulthorpe / dECOi; **24** Amanda Levete Architects / Leo Torri for DuPont™ Corian®; **25 L and M** ONL (Oosterhuis_Lénárd); **25R** Nick Dunn; **26** sixteen*(makers); **27a** Patrick Drewello / ArchiBureau; **27b and c** Nick Dunn; **27d** Timothieus Marjot; **27e and f** Nick Dunn; **28T** Nick Dunn; **28B** Tom Wiscombe / EMERGENT; **29TL** Barkow Leibinger; **29TR** Barkow Leibinger / David Franck; **29B** Studio Gang Architects / Steve Hall / Hedrich Blessing; **30** Mark Goulthorpe/dECOi; **32L** Coop Himmelb(l)au; **32R** Rogers Stirk Harbour + Partners; **33T** Joanna Szulda; **33M** Tom Wiscombe / EMERGENT; **33B** Daniel Richards; **34L** ONL (Oosterhuis_Lénárd); **34R** Rogers Stirk Harbour + Partners; **35T** Zaha Hadid Architects; **35B** Reiser + Umemoto; **36T and M** MVRDV; **36B** Foreign Office Architects; **37T and M** Tom Wiscombe / EMERGENT; **37B** Neri Oxman; **38–39** Amanda Levete Architects; **40L** ONL (Oosterhuis_Lénárd); **40R** UNStudio / Christian Richters; **41** Barkow Leibinger; **42** NOX; **43T** Patrick Drewello / ArchiBureau; **43M and B** West 8 Urban Design & Landscape Architecture B.V.; **44** Patrick Drewello / ArchiBureau; **45T** Patrick Drewello / ArchiBureau; **45B** Future Cities Lab (Johnson and Gattegno); **46–48** © PBAI; **49** Franken Architekten; **50T** Zaha Hadid Architects; **50 second from T** Zaha Hadid Architects / Werner Huthmacher; **50M** Reiser + Umemoto; **50BR** Reiser + Umemoto / Imre Solt; **51** NOX; **52** Franken Architekten; **53** Gramazio & Kohler, ETH Zurich; **54** Future Cities Lab (Johnson and Gattegno); **55** Tom Wiscombe / EMERGENT; **56–57** Zaha Hadid Architects; **58–59** Tom Wiscombe / EMERGENT; **60T and BL** Rogers Stirk Harbour + Partners; **60BR** Hayes Davidson; **61** Amanda Levete Architects; **62** Kokkugia; **63** John Dent; **64–65** Joanna Szulda; **66** Daniel Richards; **67 T** AMO/OMA; **67M and B** Phil Meech; **68–69** Romulus Sim; **70–71** Neri Oxman; **72–73** Faulders Studio / Studio M; **74** Amanda Levete Architects / Leo Torri for DuPont™ Corian®; **76L** Gramazio & Kohler, ETH Zurich; **76R** Michael Hansmeyer; **77T** Greg Lynn FORM; **77B** Amanda Levete Architects / Leo Torri for DuPont™ Corian®; **78–79** Tom Wiscombe/EMERGENT; **80–81** Future Cities Lab and Thomas Kelley (Johnson and Gattegno); **82–83** Misha Smith; **84** Timothieus Marjot; **85** Michael Hansmeyer; **86–87** Mark Goulthorpe / dECOi; **88** Kumiko Shimizu; **90** Bjarke Ingels Group (BIG); **91T and M** Zones Urbaines Sensibles (ZUS); **91B** Coop Himmelb(l)au; **92T and M** Barkow Leibinger; **92B** Rupert Griffiths; **93** sixteen*(makers); **94** Barkow Leibinger; **95T** Corinne Rose; **95M** Barkow Leibinger; **95B** David Franck; **97TL** Gramazio & Kohler, Architecture and Digital Fabrication, ETH Zurich; **97TR** Coop Himmelb(l)au; **97ML** Nick Dunn; **97MR** Future Cities Lab; **97B** Coop Himmelb(l)au; **98** John Bridge; **99** Rupert Griffiths; **100T, M and BL** Ming Chung and Nick Tyson; **100BR** Avital Wittenberg; **101** Ming Chung and Nick Tyson; **101T** S. Savoury; **0101BR** Richard Brook; **102** Zones Urbaines Sensibles (ZUS); **103T** sixteen*(makers); **103B** Paul Broadbent; **104T** Rogers Stirk Harbour + Partners; **104 M and B** Mike Fairbrass / Rogers Stirk Harbour + Partners; **105** Joanna Szulda; **106 T** Patrick Drewello / ArchiBureau; **106M and B** Adrian Bowyer; **107** Shiro Studio; **108** Coop Himmelb(l)au; **109T** Z+F UK Ltd; **109M** Coop Himmelb(l)au; **110** 3XN; **111** Gramazio & Kohler, Architecture and Digital Fabrication, ETH Zurich; **112–113** Supermanoeuvre and Matter Design; **114–115** Gramazio & Kohler, ETH Zurich; **116** 3XN; **118** Gramazio & Kohler, ETH Zurich; **119T** Gramazio & Kohler, ETH Zurich; **119M** Future Cities Lab; **119B** UNStudio / Christian Richters; **120** Studio Gang Architects / Beth Zacherle; **121** West 8 Urban Design & Landscape Architecture B.V.; **122** Faulders Studio; **123** Gramazio & Kohler, Architecture and Digital Fabrication, ETH Zurich; **124** Timothieus Marjot; **125** sixteen*(makers); **126–127** NOX; **128–129** Joanna Szulda; **130** Mark Goulthorpe / dECOi; **131** Faulders Studio; **131B** Faulders Studio / Marion Brenner; **132–133** Gramazio & Kohler, Zurich; **134–135** Amanda Levete Architects; **135 M R and B** Amanda Levete Architects / Gidon Fuehrer; **136–138** Mark Goulthorpe / dECOi; **139** ONL (Oosterhuis_Lénárd); **140 BL** Office for Metropolitan Architecture / Iwan Baan; **140BR** Office for Metropolitan Architecture; **141** UNStudio / Christian Richters; **142** Reiser + Umemoto; **143** Studio Gang Architects / Greg Murphy; **144–145** sixteen*(makers); **146–147** Tom Wiscombe / EMERGENT; **148L** Greg Lynn FORM; **148 R** 3deluxe; **149** UNStudio / Iwan Baan; **150** Mark Goulthorpe / dECOi; **151** Barkow Leibinger; **152–153** Franken Architekten; **154–155** 3deluxe; **156–157** Amo Kalsi / Rogers Stirk Harbour + Partners; **157B** Bellapart; **158** Zaha Hadid Architects; **159 T** Zaha Hadid Architects / Michelle Litvin; **159B** Zaha Hadid Architects / Thomas Gray; **160–161** Barkow Leibinger; **161B** Barkow Leibinger / Christian Richters; **162–163** Franken Architekten; **164–165** Rogers Stirk Harbour + Partners; **164T** Hayes Davidson; **164B** Expedition Engineering; **165M and B** Expedition Engineering; **166** UNStudio / Christian Richters; **167T and M** Reiser + Umemoto; **167B** Future Cities Lab (Johnson and Gattegno); **168** 3XN ; **169** Barkow Leibinger; **170** Studio Gang Architects; **171** Studio Gang Architects / Harry Zernike; **172** Faulders Studio; **173** Barkow Leibinger; **174–175** Future Cities Lab; **176** Bre Pettis / MakerBot Industries; **177** Marilena Skavara / microhappy μ:); **178–179** Gramazio & Kohler, Architecture and Digital Fabrication, ETH Zurich; **180–181** Skylar Tibbits; **182–183** Phil Ayres; **183T** Anders Ingvartsen; **184** Skylar Tibbits; **185** Neri Oxman